CONTEMPORARY ISSUES

JOBS and ECONOMY

CONTEMPORARY ISSUES

CRIMINAL JUSTICE SYSTEM
EDUCATION
THE ENVIRONMENT
GENDER EQUALITY
GUN CONTROL
HEALTH CARE
IMMIGRATION
JOBS AND ECONOMY
MENTAL HEALTH
POVERTY AND WELFARE
PRIVACY AND SOCIAL MEDIA
RACE RELATIONS
RELIGIOUS FREEDOM

CONTEMPORARY ISSUES

JOBS and ECONOMY

MARK R. WHITTINGTON

MASON CREST
450 Parkway Drive, Suite D, Broomall, Pennsylvania 19008
(866) MCP-BOOK (toll-free) • www.masoncrest.com

© 2020 by Mason Crest, an imprint of National Highlights, Inc.

All rights reserved. No part of this publication may be reproduced or transmitted in any form or by any means, electronic or mechanical, including photocopying, recording, taping, or any information storage and retrieval system, without permission from the publisher.

Printed and bound in the United States of America.

CPSIA Compliance Information: Batch #CCRI2019.
For further information, contact Mason Crest at 1-866-MCP-Book.

First printing
1 3 5 7 9 8 6 4 2

ISBN (hardback) 978-1-4222-4395-4
ISBN (series) 978-1-4222-4387-9
ISBN (ebook) 978-1-4222-7410-1

Library of Congress Cataloging-in-Publication Data
on file at the Library of Congress

Interior and cover design: Torque Advertising + Design
Production: Michelle Luke

Publisher's Note: Websites listed in this book were active at the time of publication. The publisher is not responsible for websites that have changed their address or discontinued operation since the date of publication. The publisher reviews and updates the websites each time the book is reprinted.

QR CODES AND LINKS TO THIRD-PARTY CONTENT

You may gain access to certain third-party content ("Third-Party Sites") by scanning and using the QR Codes that appear in this publication (the "QR Codes"). We do not operate or control in any respect any information, products, or services on such Third-Party Sites linked to by us via the QR Codes included in this publication, and we assume no responsibility for any materials you may access using the QR Codes. Your use of the QR Codes may be subject to terms, limitations, or restrictions set forth in the applicable terms of use or otherwise established by the owners of the Third-Party Sites. Our linking to such Third-Party Sites via the QR Codes does not imply an endorsement or sponsorship of such Third-Party Sites or the information, products, or services offered on or through the Third-Party Sites, nor does it imply an endorsement or sponsorship of this publication by the owners of such Third-Party Sites.

CONTENTS

Chapter 1: Managing a Modern Economy 7
Chapter 2: Do Lower Taxes Stimulate Economic Activity?......... 27
Chapter 3: Should Infrastructure Investments Be Privatized? .. 47
Chapter 4: How Heavily Should Government Invest
 In Science and Technology Research?..................... 65
Chapter 5: Does Deregulation Help or Hurt
 Workers and the Economy? 83
Series Glossary of Key Terms 100
Organizations to Contact 101
Further Reading... 102
Internet Resources.. 102
Chapter Notes 103
Index... 108
Author's Biography and Credits... 112

KEY ICONS TO LOOK FOR:

Words to Understand: These words with their easy-to-understand definitions will increase the reader's understanding of the text while building vocabulary skills.

Sidebars: This boxed material within the main text allows readers to build knowledge, gain insights, explore possibilities, and broaden their perspectives by weaving together additional information to provide realistic and holistic perspectives.

Educational videos: Readers can view videos by scanning our QR codes, providing them with additional educational content to supplement the text. Examples include news coverage, moments in history, speeches, iconic sports moments, and much more!

Text-Dependent Questions: These questions send the reader back to the text for more careful attention to the evidence presented there.

Research Projects: Readers are pointed toward areas of further inquiry connected to each chapter. Suggestions are provided for projects that encourage deeper research and analysis.

Series Glossary of Key Terms: This back-of-the-book glossary contains terminology used throughout this series. Words found here increase the reader's ability to read and comprehend higher-level books and articles in this field.

WORDS TO UNDERSTAND

capitalism—an economic system in which production and trade are controlled by private business.

mixed economy—an economic system in which both private business and the government provide goods and service.

social democracy—a system of government in which, while production and trade are controlled primarily by private business, massive interventions by the government are used to promote fairness, security, and social justice.

socialism—an economic system in which production and trade are controlled by the government.

MANAGING A MODERN ECONOMY

CHAPTER 1

Politicians and public policy experts, no matter what their political persuasion, agree that they want people to have jobs and for the economy to grow at a healthy and sustainable rate. However, they disagree considerably about how to achieve these goals.

Adam Smith, an eighteenth-century Scottish economist and philosopher, was an early proponent of free market **capitalism**. In his book *The Wealth of Nations*, which was published in 1776, the same year the American Revolution began, described the interaction of producers and consumers as "the invisible hand."

> [The rich] consume little more than the poor, and in spite of their natural selfishness and rapacity...they divide with the poor the produce of all their improvements. They are led by an invisible hand to make nearly the same distribution of the necessaries of life, which would have been made, had the earth been divided into equal portions among all its inhabitants, and thus without intending it, without knowing it, advance the interest of the society, and afford means to the multiplication of the species.[1]

In other words, according to Smith, unrestrained capitalism will always tend to create the most good and

> "Indeed, a major source of objection to a free economy is precisely that it… gives people what they want instead of what a particular group thinks they ought to want. Underlying most arguments against the free market is a lack of belief in freedom itself."[2]
> —Milton Friedman, American economist and Nobel Prize winner

the fairest distribution of wealth. Competition causes businesses to constantly improve their goods and services and to lower their prices so that more customers can afford them.

While the roots of **socialism** can be found as early as the French Revolution, Karl Marx, a nineteenth-century German philosopher, is considered the father of the modern version of that approach to economics as well as of communism. Marx stated that, "The theory of communism can be summed up in one sentence. Abolish all private property."[3] Marx meant that under communism, all property would be collectively owned and controlled by the people, through a central government.

Communism has fallen out of favor since the collapse of the Soviet Union in the early 1990s. However, socialism, which Marx saw as a transition phase between capitalism and communism, is alive and well, to a certain extent. Socialism has been practiced differently in different places and times in history.

After World War II, socialists in western nations distinguished themselves from communists by adhering to democratic principles. Great Britain, for example, practiced a form of socialism between 1945 and 1951, when the Labour Party won a majority in parliament. The Labour

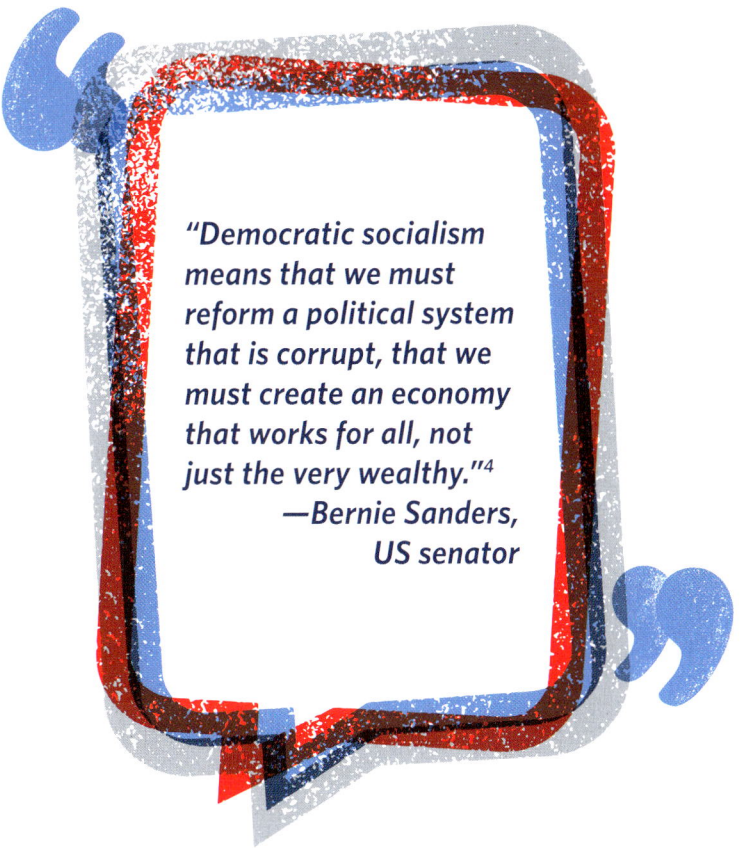

"Democratic socialism means that we must reform a political system that is corrupt, that we must create an economy that works for all, not just the very wealthy."[4]
—Bernie Sanders, US senator

government established a national health care system and implemented public control over major industries and utilities. However, when the Labour Party lost power, it peacefully turned over control of the government to the victorious Conservative Party. Britain would eventually divest itself of many state-owned industries, such as railroads and the coal industry, during the 1980s when Margaret Thatcher served as prime minister.

A crowd attends a 2018 rally to hear Social Democrat and Prime Minister Stefan Löfven speak in Umeå, Sweden. The Social Democratic Party is the largest and oldest political party in Sweden.

Scandinavian countries, such as Sweden, Denmark, and Norway, are often described as socialist. However, the truth is a little more complicated. These countries have created **mixed economies**, in which the governments allow people to own private businesses, but impose heavy taxes in return for a generous program of social services, including health care, education, and cradle-to-grave welfare. Because the governments are democratically elected by the people in elections that are free and fair, these countries are best described as **social democracies**, rather than socialist.

The closest to something resembling pure capitalism took place during the first century or so of the United States. However, this state of affairs began to change with the beginning of the Progressive Era in the late nineteenth century. The Progressives were people who believed that

To learn more about the origins of capitalism, scan here.

Managing a Modern Economy

the problems of society—such as poverty, violence, greed, racism, and class warfare—could be addressed by providing better education and safer, fairer workplaces. They felt that it was the government's job to ensure these conditions were met.

"Social reformers like Jane Addams and journalists like Jacob Riis and Ida Tarbell were powerful voices for progressivism. They concentrated on exposing the evils of corporate greed, combating fear of immigrants, and urging Americans to think hard about what democracy meant," notes an article from George Washington University. "On a national level, progressivism gained a strong voice in the White House when Theodore Roosevelt became president in 1901. TR believed that strong corporations were good for America, but he also believed that corporate behavior must be watched to ensure that corporate greed did not get out of hand (trust-busting and federal regulation of business)."[5]

One of the institutions created by Progressives during the early years of the twentieth century was the Federal Reserve, a central bank designed to control the supply of money in the United States. The purpose of this central bank was to control the rate of price inflation and to keep the economy growing at a steady rate. The modern income tax was also created by the progressives.

After the First World War ended in 1918, the United States experienced an economic boom that lasted for much of the 1920s. However, in 1929 the stock market crashed,

Theodore Roosevelt speaks to a crowd in New York. As president, Roosevelt sought to regulate certain industries—including railroads, meatpackers, and steel companies—to ensure competition and protect the public.

sparking a sharp decline in US economic productivity. Within a year the entire world was affected by a global economic downturn known as the Great Depression. Businesses and factories were closed, and millions of people lost their jobs and could not find work.

In 1933, newly elected President Franklin Roosevelt attempted to alleviate the effects of the Great Depression by implementing a series of programs that would stabilize the economy, create jobs, and provide assistance for those who were suffering. Roosevelt's programs became known as the New Deal. "Over the next eight years, the government instituted a series of experimental New Deal projects and programs, such as the CCC, the WPA, the TVA, the SEC and others, that aimed to restore some measure of dignity and prosperity to many Americans," notes the History Channel. "Roosevelt's New Deal

Heavy equipment is used to construct a hydroelectric dam as part of the Tennessee Valley Authority (TVA). This was a government agency created as part of Franklin D. Roosevelt's New Deal to develop the southern part of the poor farming region known as Appalachia.

fundamentally and permanently changed the federal government's relationship with U.S. citizens."[6]

Today's system of Social Security, which provides monthly payments for older Americans as well as those who cannot work because of a disability, is a product of the New Deal. So are agricultural subsidies and many economic regulations that persist to this day. Additionally, much of the power-generating infrastructure created by the Tennessee Valley Authority and similar government agencies still exists.

Another wave of government intervention in the economy took place during the 1960s. The "War on Poverty" was part of President Lyndon B. Johnson's Great Society program designed to create a more prosperous, fairer America. A goal of the project was to help underprivileged Americans break the cycle of poverty by receiving an education or developing job skills.

"Johnson tasked state and local governments with creating work training programs for up to 200,000 men and women," notes the History Channel.

> A national work-study program was also established to offer 140,000 Americans the chance to go to college who could otherwise not afford it. Other initiatives the so-called War on Poverty offered were: a Community Action program for people to tackle poverty within their own communities; the ability for the government to recruit and train skilled American volunteers to serve poverty-stricken communities; loans and guarantees for employers who offered jobs to the unemployed; funds for farmers to purchase land and establish agricultural co-ops; and help for unemployed parents preparing to enter the workforce.[7]

Johnson's successor, President Richard Nixon, continued the practice of government intervention in the economy with the establishment of new agencies such as the Occupational Safety and Health Administration (OSHA) and the Environmental Protection Agency (EPA). Nixon even attempted to establish government control over wages and prices, but this approach failed.

TAX REDUCTION

Since the end of World War II in 1945, US presidents have tried many things to stimulate the economy and

MEASURING ECONOMIC FREEDOM

According to 2019 Index of Economic Freedom, the Chinese city of Hong Kong is considered the most economically free in the world. Although Hong Kong has been under the control of the communist government of China since 1997, the city has been allowed a certain degree of autonomy not available to other parts of China. As a result, Hong Kong's economic freedom score is 90.2, well above the regional and world averages.

"An exceptionally competitive financial and business hub, Hong Kong remains one of the world's most resilient economies," notes the Heritage create jobs. Some have cut taxes and reduced government regulations, believing that easing the burdens that government impose on private business would encourage more economic activity. The free market, unimpeded by taxes and government regulations, is thought best suited to grow the economy and create jobs.

John F. Kennedy was the first president after World War II to propose across-the-board tax cuts. JFK presented his plan to the Economic Club of New York in a speech delivered on December 14, 1962, along with proposals for more education and investments in technology. "The final and best means of strengthening demand among consumers and business is to reduce the burden on private income and the deterrents to private initiative which are imposed by our present tax system—and this

Foundation, which produces the index. "A high-quality legal framework provides effective protection of property rights and strongly supports the rule of law. There is little tolerance for corruption, and a high degree of transparency enhances government integrity. Regulatory efficiency and openness to global commerce undergird a vibrant entrepreneurial climate. Hong Kong's economic linkage with the mainland is most evident in the finance and trading sectors."[8]

By comparison, the United States is ranked twelfth on the 2019 Index of Economic Freedom, with a score of 76.8.

President Lyndon B. Johnson signs the Economic Opportunity Act, August 1964. The legislation was the centerpiece of Johnson's "War on Poverty," and was intended to provide education, job training, and other assistance to low-income Americans.

administration pledged itself last summer to an across-the-board, top-to-bottom cut in personal and corporate income taxes to be enacted and become effective in 1963."[9]

It fell to Kennedy's successor, President Lyndon Johnson, to enact the Kennedy tax cuts, which lowered the tax rates by approximately 20 percent, lowered the corporate tax rate, and instituted the first minimum standard deduction. The tax cut, usually favored by free market conservatives, was enacted at the same time as LBJ's more government-centric War on Poverty programs.

A famous attempt to use tax cuts to stimulate the economy took place during the early years of the Reagan administration. America's economy had been in the doldrums for a while when Ronald Reagan came to office in 1981. An across-the-board tax cut of 25 percent, phased in over three years, was his prescription to get America's economy moving again. In 1986, President Reagan proposed another tax reform measure that flattened tax rates, while eliminating a number of deductions and shelters. "The Tax Reform Act of 1986 lowered the top tax rate for ordinary income from 50 percent to 28 percent and raised the bottom tax rate from 11 percent to 15 percent," notes an Investopedia article. "This was the first time in U.S. income tax history that the top tax rate was lowered and the bottom rate was increased at the same time."[10] The tax reform was passed with bipartisan support in Congress.

In 2001, and again in 2003, President George W. Bush enacted additional across-the-board tax cuts, citing the then surpluses the federal government was running as an argument for doing so. The 2001 law reduced individual tax rates and repealed the estate tax. The 2003 law cut taxes on dividends and extended the individual tax cuts from the 2001 law. Bush's tax cuts were set to expire after a ten-year period. However in 2012 his successor, President Barack Obama, signed a provision that made most of the Bush tax cuts permanent, other than the ones for the highest earners.

The most recent government tax cut package took place in 2017 under President Donald Trump. Tax rates were cut again, and the standard deduction was greatly increased, making filing taxes much simpler for many people. However, as the *CPA Journal* notes, "Most of the provisions for individuals are temporary; they expire after 2025 unless Congress takes further action."[11]

GOVERNMENT REGULATIONS AND INVESTMENTS

Regulatory relief is another way that the governments try to effect economic growth. As the Cato Institute once noted, "Because the costs imposed by federal regulations are so huge (exceeding the budgets of all the domestic discretionary spending programs of the federal government), every president from Gerald Ford to Bill Clinton has established a formal system to review new government regulations before they are issued. Each of those efforts has involved units of the Executive Office of the President, with the specifics varying over a fairly modest range of differences."[12]

As president, Ronald Reagan raised corporate income taxes in 1982 to help bring the economy out of a recession. In 1986, he oversaw major changes to the tax code that significantly reduced tax rates, particularly for the highest income earners.

Deregulation—the process of eliminating government regulations on certain industries—is another form of regulatory relief. Between the 1930s and the early 1970s, the US government imposed rules and regulations that restricted on how industries could operate, generally to protect workers and consumers from exploitation. However, supporters of deregulation believe that government regulations stop people from investing in

Managing a Modern Economy

those industries, limiting their opportunities for growth. They argue that deregulation will help consumers by allowing more competition.

Beginning in the 1970s, US leaders began to deregulate certain industries, including rail and air transportation,

Many economists believe that deregulation of mortgage banks created the conditions for a serious financial crisis that began in 2007-08 with the collapse of the subprime mortgage industry. The crisis resulted in the loss of nearly 9 million US jobs, as well as $19.2 trillion in household wealth, according to the US Department of the Treasury.

telecommunication, and finance. The deregulation of the banking industry contributed to a booming stock market in the 1990s and early 2000s. However, loosening the rules that governed financial companies allowed them to take greater risks, which resulted in the subprime mortgage crisis of 2007 and a financial crash the following year. New regulations were imposed in 2010 with the Dodd-Frank Act, which restricted subprime mortgage lending and derivatives trading. Nevertheless, the Trump administration seems to favor additional deregulation.

Government science and technology investments are often a by-product of military research. In 1915, during the Wilson Administration, the National Advisory Committee on Aeronautics was created to promote research into aeronautical technology. In the 1950s NACA evolved into the National Aeronautics and Space Administration (NASA), which continues aeronautical research and development as well as space technology, science, and exploration. During and after World War II, government researchers made a series of innovations in aviation, rocketry, communications, navigation, and medicine. The Internet that we use today was originally created as a project of the US Department of Defense in the 1960s, to allow computers at different universities to share information.

Other government agencies involved in science and technology research include the Department of Energy Office of Science, the National Science Foundation, and the National Institutes of Health, among many others. While some disagree how research and development money should be spent, government-funded research and development enjoys wide bipartisan support.

Today, Americans hold two divergent world-views concerning the best way to help the economy and create jobs. The free market view suggests that the government can best grow the economy and jobs by leaving private business alone as much as possible. The big government view, on the other hand, argues that government action, both direct and indirect, best serves the United States' economic health. Tension between these two approaches defines American politics. The essays that follow in this book will give you some insights into the pros and cons of each approach.

TEXT-DEPENDENT QUESTIONS

1. What did Adam Smith mean by the "invisible hand?"
2. What were some accomplishments of the Progressives?
3. What two government agencies were created by President Richard Nixon to manage economic activity?
4. What is the principal argument for deregulation?

RESEARCH PROJECTS

Research the economic effects of the New Deal. Did the various government programs and initiatives of the 1930s have a lasting, beneficial effect on the American economy? Explain why or why not in a two-page paper, using data to support your conclusions. Share your report with the class.

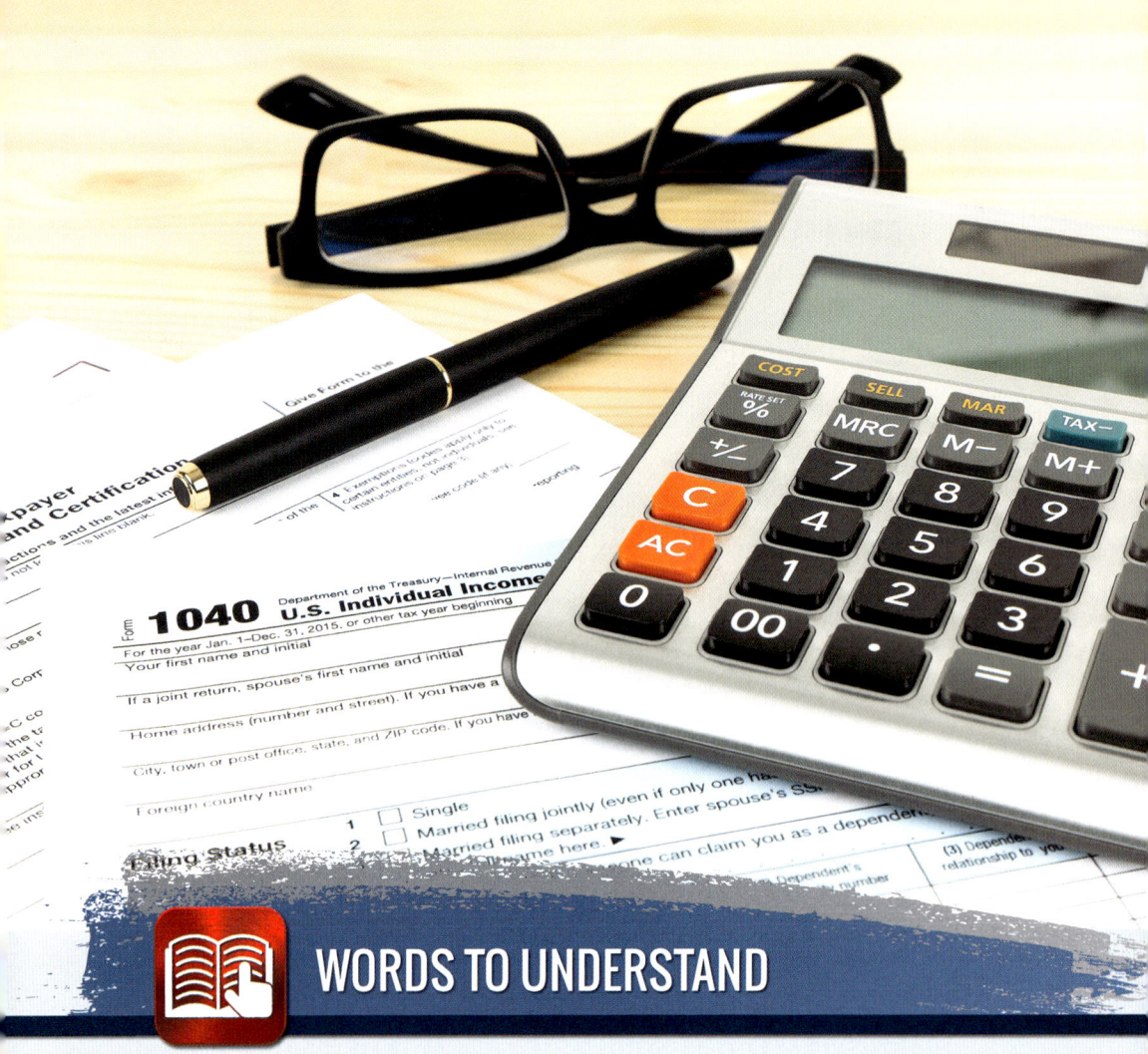

WORDS TO UNDERSTAND

business taxes—taxes levied on profits derived from a business.

income taxes—taxes levied as a percentage of income, including wages, interest, dividends, and capital gains.

Internal Revenue Service—the agency of the federal government charged with collecting taxes and enforcing the tax laws.

property taxes—taxes levied on the amount of property one owns, usually a home or business.

sales taxes—taxes as a percentage of a good or service sold. Usually levied by the vendor selling the good or service.

DO LOWER TAXES STIMULATE ECONOMIC ACTIVITY?

CHAPTER 2

Americans have long harbored a special dislike of taxes. Indeed, it can be safely said that the American Revolution began when a group of angry colonists dumped cases of tea into Boston Harbor in December 1773 to protest the British tax on that popular beverage. Benjamin Franklin, one of the architects of the Revolution, famously said, "In this world nothing can be said to be certain, except death and taxes."[13] The twentieth-century humorist Will Rogers noted, "The only difference between death and taxes is that death does not get worse every time Congress meets."[14]

Americans are obliged to pay taxes to support federal, state, and local governments. These taxes include federal and state **income taxes**, Social Security taxes, Medicare taxes, **property taxes**, **sales taxes**, and a variety of **business taxes**, the cost of which businesses generally pass on to the consumer.

Some taxes are easy to pay. Sales taxes are transparent, because they are included in the cost of a good or service. Most homeowners get a bill for their annual property taxes at the start or end of each year.

It can be very difficult for people to comply with federal and state requirements for reporting income for tax purposes. An entire industry of tax preparation specialists and accountants has arisen to help people navigate through the various deductions, exemptions, and other formulas that must be understood in order to report their income and pay the state and federal taxes they owe. Computer programs are also available to help taxpayers comply with the tax code.

No one wants to tangle with the **Internal Revenue Service**, even as a result of an honest mistake. Interest and penalties, along with threats of wage garnishment, make the IRS one of the most feared agencies in the federal government.

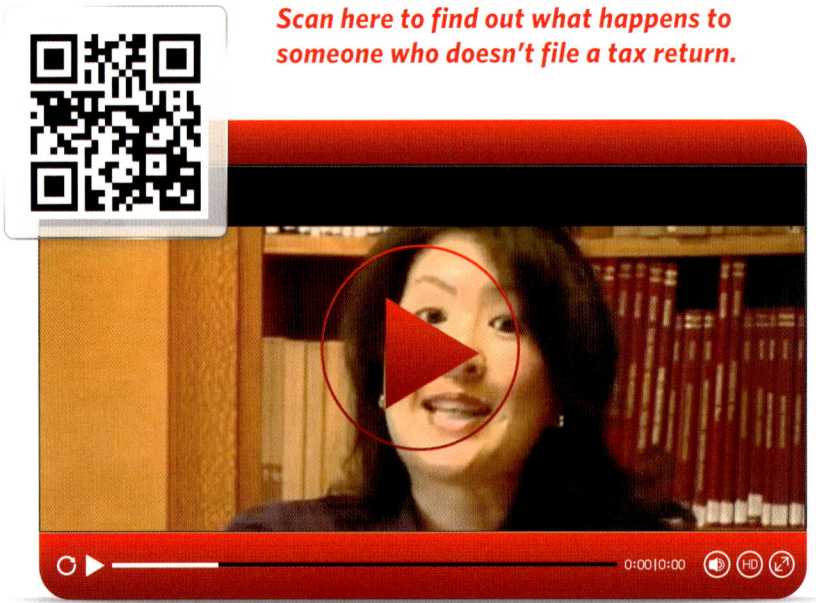

Scan here to find out what happens to someone who doesn't file a tax return.

The federal income tax is designed to be "progressive," which means that people who make different incomes are assessed a different rate. Investopedia explains:

> The federal income tax is built on a progressive tax system, where higher income earners are taxed at a higher rate. Taxpayers who earn below an annual threshold set by the government would pay little to no tax, while workers who earn six figures or more annually have a mandatory tax rate that applies to their income. The tax rate that applies to each individual is set up in a marginal tax bracket that shows the highest tax rate to be paid on income earned. In effect, the amount of taxable income that one earns determines which tax bracket he would fall into."[15]

Because of the many ways that Americans are taxed, most Americans have only a vague idea of exactly how much they actually pay in taxes each year. The amount can vary depending on where a person lives, the person's income and other assets, and even the skill of their tax accountant. According to 2018 data, Montana residents pay the lowest taxes, at an average of about $7,000 per person annually. Delaware and West Virginia also have very low tax rates. On the other side, the three states with the highest taxes are New Jersey (nearly $20,000 a year on average), New York, and California.

Political elites disagree not only over how high or low taxes should be, but also on what should be taxed. On occasion, a proposal to lower taxes across the board is offered as a way to boost the economy and to create more jobs.

LOWER TAXES LEAD TO JOBS AND ECONOMIC GROWTH

In 2001, when President George W. Bush proposed his first round of tax cuts, economist David Boaz of the Cato Institute explained why tax cuts are necessary. "High taxes discourage work and investment," wrote Boaz. "Taxes create a 'wedge' between what the employer pays and what the employee receives, so some jobs don't get created. High marginal tax rates also discourage people from working overtime or from making new investments.... Most economists now agree that a reduction in marginal tax rates will increase output to some degree."[16]

At the time they were passed in 2003, the Bush-era tax cuts were controversial. Some analysts claimed that they would damage the economy. However, later research showed that this was far from the case. In fact, in an article in *American Thinker*, Andrew Foy and Brenton Stransky found that the effect was quite the opposite. "So what was the effect of the Bush tax cuts?" they wrote. "The data reveals that tax revenues in 2006 were actually $47 billion above the levels projected by the Congressional Budget Office before the 2003 tax cuts. Clearly, tax rates were beyond the point of equilibrium.

"The Bush tax cuts were intended to increase market incentives to work, save, and invest and thus create jobs and increase economic growth. An analysis of the six quarters before and after the 2003 tax cuts shows that this is exactly what happened."[17]

This of course was not the first time that lowering

President George W. Bush delivers his State of the Union speech before a joint session of Congress. Tax cuts passed in 2001 and 2003 lowered the marginal tax rates for nearly all US taxpayers.

Do Lower Taxes Stimulate Economic Activity?

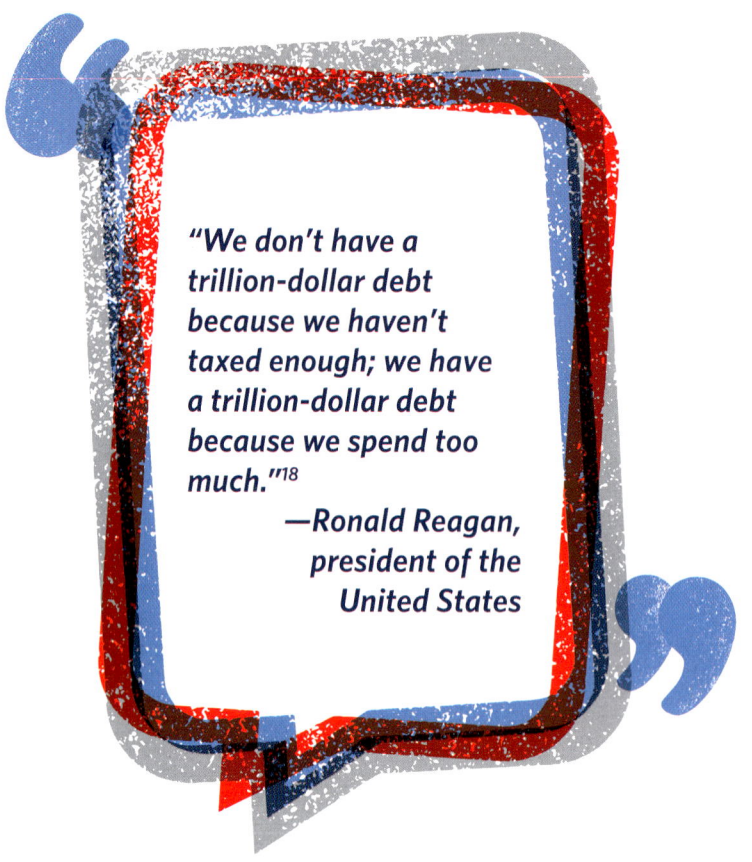

"We don't have a trillion-dollar debt because we haven't taxed enough; we have a trillion-dollar debt because we spend too much."[18]

—Ronald Reagan, president of the United States

taxes resulted in economic growth. In the late 1970s, the American economy went into a steep recession. The decline in economic growth occurred simultaneously with high rates of monetary inflation: a phenomena known as stagflation.

After being elected president in 1980, Ronald Reagan commissioned a council of economic advisors, led by Milton Friedman, to study the problem. They recommended lower tax rates, along with changes to the Federal Reserve's policies regarding interest rates. In August 1981, President Reagan signed the Economic

Recovery Tax Act, which reduced income tax rates for individuals and provided other tax incentives for small businesses and private savings. The recovery took some time, but by 1983 the American economy was growing at a steady rate.

Reagan continued to support tax cuts. In 1986, the Tax Reform Act involved major changes to tax laws. The new legislation made American income tax rates for corporations and individuals lower than any other major industrialized country. According to the Reagan Foundation, the tax cuts during President Reagan's term (1981–1989) saved the average American family of four nearly $9,000 in taxes in 1987 over what that family would have paid in 1980. In addition, despite the negative effect of the economic recession that was ongoing when Reagan took office, during the eight-year term about 3 million jobs were added to the American economy.

"The numbers tell the story," notes the Foundation:

> Over the eight years of the Reagan Administration, 20 million new jobs were created. Inflation dropped from 13.5 percent in 1980 to 4.1 percent by 1988. Unemployment fell from 7.6 percent to 5.5 percent. Net worth of families earning between $20,000 and $50,000 annually grew by 27 percent. Real gross national product rose 26 percent. The prime interest rate was slashed by more than half, from an unprecedented 21.5 percent in January 1981 to 10 percent in August 1988.[19]

The Cato Institute's David Mitchell also offered a defense of the Reagan 1981 tax cuts. "We can draw some conclusions by looking at how low-tax economies such as Singapore and Hong Kong outperform the United States," noted Mitchell in a 2017 essay. "Or we can compare growth in the United States with the economic stagnation in high-tax Europe. We can also compare growth during the Reagan years with the economic malaise of the 1970s. Moreover, there's lots of academic evidence showing that lower tax

WHAT IS A FLAT TAX?

From time to time over the years, a proposal to completely remake the American tax code by implementing a flat tax has been raised. The tax code is extremely complex, with a variety of deductions, credits, or exemptions available to taxpayers. Under a flat tax plan, households would receive only one exemption, based on family size. The taxpayers would then pay a low rate on any income above that exemption level.

The theory behind a flat tax is that it would eliminate the burden of complying with the federal tax code. Supporters of a flat tax claim that a person's taxes could be filled out on a postcard in a few minutes.

"Compared to traditional tax systems, a flat tax is extremely simple," notes the Heritage Foundation. "[Taxpayers] do not need to worry about reporting dividends, interest and other forms of business/capital income. Those forms of income are taxed at rates lead to better economic performance. The bottom line is that people respond to incentives. When tax rates climb, there's more 'deadweight loss' in the economy. So when tax rates fall, output increases."[20]

It's not just Republicans who have passed tax cuts. Democratic presidents from John F. Kennedy to Barack Obama have proposed tax-reduction measures In 1963, President Kennedy proposed legislation that would lower

the business level, thus obviating any need to tax them at the individual level, since that would violate the principle of no double taxation.

"How would a flat tax work for businesses? All businesses, from the largest multinational to a corner pub, would play by the same rules. Companies would add up their receipts (how much revenue came in) and then subtract their costs (salaries, cost of raw materials, and expenses for new tools and machinery). This would give them their taxable income, which would be taxed at the low rate."[21]

A few US states, including Colorado, Pennsylvania, and Utah, use a flat tax on state residents' income. Businessman Steve Forbes made a flat tax proposal a centerpiece of his campaigns for the Republican Party's presidential nomination in 1996 and 2000. More recently, before the 2016 election Republican candidates Ben Carson, Ted Cruz, and Rand Paul all discussed plans to replace the progressive income tax with a flat tax.

President Barack Obama extended the Bush tax cuts, making most of the cuts permanent with the American Taxpayer Relief Act of 2012.

the highest tax rate on personal income over $100,000 (equivalent to about $800,000 in 2019 dollars) from 91 percent to 70 percent, and lowered the corporate tax rate from 52 percent to 48 percent. The legislation was passed after Kennedy's assassination as the Revenue Act of 1964.

In an essay in *Market Watch*, economist Diana Furchtgott-Roth pointed out the benefits of Kennedy's changes. "After the tax cuts, real GDP grew at 5.8 percent in 1964, 6.5 percent in 1965, and 6.6 percent in 1966," wrote Furchtgott-Roth. "The unemployment rate declined from 5.2 percent in 1964 to 3.8 percent in 1966, falling all the way to 3.5 percent in 1969. Although Kennedy did not live to see it, the rest of us did."[22]

Proponents of using tax cuts to grow the economy and jobs claim that leaving more money in individuals' pockets and businesses spurs such growth. People have more money to spend on goods and services and to save for new homes, college education, and retirement. Businesses have more money to invest in plants and equipment, Supporters of tax cuts would seem to have some statistics from real-world tax-cut initiatives to buttress their claims.

On a higher level, those who advocate for tax cuts claim a moral imperative. People earn money by their own labor and initiative and should be allowed to keep as much as possible. Governments tend to waste money on dubious projects, whereas private individuals and businesses will save and spend it productively, fulfilling Adam Smith's "invisible hand" principle.

CUTTING TAXES MAINLY BENEFITS THE WEALTHY

Arguments against across-the-board tax cuts to stimulate the economy tend to fall into two categories. One group of opponents claims that such tax cuts favor only the wealthy at the expense of the middle class and poor. Another group maintains that such tax cuts explode the deficit, causing the long-term national debt to increase to unsustainable levels.

Senator Bernie Sanders, an independent from Vermont who was a candidate for president in 2016 and 2020, is firmly in the first camp. In an interview with Real Clear Politics, he spoke about the Trump administration's 2017 tax cut proposal. He believed that the cuts would increase the budget deficit, and force future Congresses to cut spending on essential programs. "This is legislation written for wealthy campaign contributors," complained Sanders. "After you raise the deficit by $1.4 trillion, you're going to come back and cut Social Security, Medicare, Medicaid, education, and the needs of working families. What kind of decency is there when we have legislation giving massive tax breaks to billionaires, and then comes back and wants to cut Social Security and Medicaid? This bill must not pass."[23]

Often proponents of tax cuts claim that the reductions will pay for themselves because of increased revenue to do more economic activity. The Brookings Institute has analyzed the 1981 Reagan tax cuts, and found that the promised increase in tax revenues never actually

In his first year as president, Donald Trump signed a major tax reform program into law. However, most experts believe the Tax Cuts and Jobs Act of 2017 will increase the federal budget deficit, and that most of the benefits go to the wealthiest Americans.

materialized. "When Ronald Reagan arrived in Washington in 1981, circumstances were very different than they are today," write Alan Auerbach and William Gale. "Inflation was nearly 10 percent. The Federal Reserve had pushed interest rates into double digits. The federal debt was about half what it is today, measured as a share of the economy. The Reagan tax cut was huge. The top rate fell from 70 percent to 50 percent. The tax cut didn't pay for itself. According to later Treasury estimates, it reduced

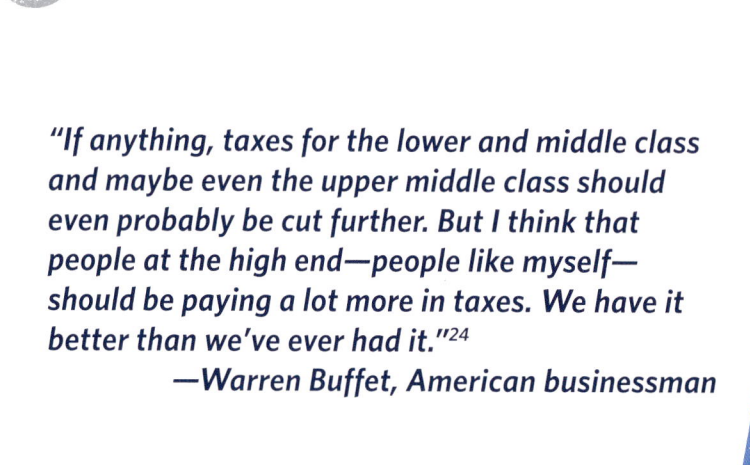

> "If anything, taxes for the lower and middle class and maybe even the upper middle class should even probably be cut further. But I think that people at the high end—people like myself—should be paying a lot more in taxes. We have it better than we've ever had it."[24]
> —Warren Buffet, American businessman

federal revenues by about 9 percent in the first couple of years. In fact, most of the top Reagan administration officials didn't think the tax cut would pay for itself. They were counting on spending cuts to avoid blowing up the deficit. But they never materialized."[25]

Auerbach and Gale went on to suggest, after an analysis of the 1986 tax reform bill, that tax cuts are just one way that the government can affect the economy. "One lesson from this: Despite all the rhetoric over the economic effects of big tax bills, taxes are only one of many factors that drive the economy—and probably not as big a factor as you'd think when listening to the debate when those bills are pending in Congress."[26]

The term "bull market" refers to a period when the economy is strong, marked by an increase in the prices of corporate stocks. This statue of a charging bull, symbolizing the aggression and opportunity of the bull market, is located near the New York Stock Exchange on Wall Street.

Do Lower Taxes Stimulate Economic Activity?

People advocating tax cuts, in other words, have to pay attention to those many factors, which include federal spending and interest rates, the latter of which is affected by the Federal Reserve. The Fed's actions to end inflation resulted in sky-high interest rates in the early 1980s and thus wiped out some of the stimulative effects of the 1981 tax cuts.

At one time, conservatives tended to favor a balanced budget over tax cuts. If taxes were to be cut at all, then they had to be balanced with spending cuts to keep the deficit from exploding. Many critics claimed that the 1981 Reagan tax cuts increased the federal deficit, making a tax increase that was passed in 1983 necessary.

The federal government is not the only entity that cuts taxes in order to stimulate the economy. Some states do so as well. For example. Kansas cut its state income tax in 2012 and 2013. The Center on Budget and Policy Priorities took a dim view of the effectiveness of this measure, however. "The deep income cuts that Kansas enacted in 2012 and 2013 for many business owners and other high-income Kansans failed to achieve their goal of boosting business formation and job creation, and lawmakers substantially repealed the tax cuts earlier this year. Former supporters have offered explanations for this failure to prevent the Kansas experience from discrediting 'supply-side' economic strategies more broadly. But the evidence does not support these explanations. Rather, the Kansas experience adds to the already compelling evidence that cutting taxes does not improve state economic performance."[27]

The case against tax cuts to stimulate the economy and grow jobs, opponents claim, is that they tend to increase income disparity by favoring the rich, people who earn high incomes and therefore pay more taxes. They also

In 2018 US Congresswoman Alexandria Ocasio-Cortez suggested a tax rate of 70 percent on the wealthiest Americans, to support her "Green New Deal" proposal for legislation to combat climate change and provide opportunity to the disadvantaged.

believe that tax cuts, far from paying for themselves, tend to explode budget deficits, increasing the national debt, which has serious long-term implications for American economic health. Opponents maintain that tax cuts without corresponding spending cuts are folly. The problem, of course, is that cutting spending has tended to be far less popular than cutting taxes.

Many opponents, especially on the left, oppose spending cuts to social programs as a matter of political ideology. Indeed, as newly elected Rep. Alexandria Ocasio-Cortez, a Democrat from New York who describes herself as a "democratic socialist" advocates, tax rates should be raised to as much as 70 percent for high earners in order to pay for new government programs they favor, such as Bernie Sanders's proposed "Medicare for All" health care program, or her own "Green New Deal" proposal to provide green energy jobs. Taxes and spending need to be increased, these politicians claim, to help the economy and increase job growth. The fight between that view and those of tax cutters is a serious division in American politics.

TEXT-DEPENDENT QUESTIONS

1. What are some types of taxes that Americans pay?
2. Which three American states have the lowest tax burden? Which states have the highest tax burden?
3. What is the "moral case" for cutting taxes?

RESEARCH PROJECTS

Starting from scratch, design a new income tax code for the United States. Figure out rates, deductions, and other factors. Defend your approach from the standpoint of revenues that could be raised and other factors such as fairness.

WORDS TO UNDERSTAND

infrastructure—the basic physical facilities and systems that serve the running of a country or other region. Examples include roads, bridges, sea ports, airports, railroads, and other things that facilitate the movement of goods and services. In the modern age, the Internet could be defined as infrastructure.

internal improvement—a nineteenth century term used to define infrastructure paid for by the federal government or by a state government.

shovel-ready project—term used to described an infrastructure construction project that has already completed the planning stages and is ready to proceed immediately once funding is authorized.

SHOULD INFRASTRUCTURE INVESTMENTS BE PRIVATIZED?

CHAPTER 3

Without roads, bridges, water and sewer systems, and an electrical grid, modern societies could not function. However, the political question has always been, how much and in what ways should the federal government be involved in the building of such facilities? The question dates back to the country's founding.

During the years from the end of the Revolution in 1783 until the American Civil War began in 1861, a series of public works was undertaken in the newly formed United States. These projects were known as **internal improvements**, and were mainly to create transportation infrastructure: roads, turnpikes, canals, harbors, and navigation improvements. Improving the country's natural advantages by developing better transportation networks was, in the eyes of George Washington, Henry Clay, and other American leaders during this time, a duty incumbent both on governments and on private corporations.

"While the need for inland transportation improvements was universally recognized, there were great differences over the questions of how these should be planned, funded, developed, and constructed," notes an article on the website

American History. "Also, with various routes available, questions of where these improvements should be made, and by whom, the federal government, the individual states, or their localities, became the basis of political and regional contention. Federal assistance for 'internal improvements' evolved slowly and haphazardly; it became the product of contentious congressional factions and an executive branch generally concerned with avoiding 'unconstitutional federal intrusions into state affairs.'"[28]

While most people recognized that infrastructure was of economic benefit, these internal improvements were usually a responsibility of the states. The Erie Canal, which linked the Hudson River to Lake Erie, was a project undertaken by New York State. It drastically shortened the time it took to transport goods between the port at New

Scan here to learn how the Erie Canal transformed New York State.

Construction of the Hoover Dam was a major infrastructure project that occurred during the 1930s. The dam cost $49 million (the equivalent of over $650 million today). The hydroelectric dam generates power for people in Nevada, Arizona, and California.

Should Infrastructure Investments Be Privatized?

York City and the Great Lakes. From there, the goods could be shipped down the Mississippi River and transported throughout the western frontier regions. The Erie Canal was a major success that made New York the most important commercial center in the young nation.

The federal government also financed some infrastructure projects. One of these was the Cumberland Road, also known as the National Road, which connected Cumberland, Maryland, and Vandalia, Illinois. The road facilitated the westward movement of thousands of settlers. Later, the federal government would pay

HIGH-TECH INFRASTRUCTURE

Sometimes infrastructure can go beyond the usual roads and bridges into projects that could seem to be science fiction. Elon Musk, the CEO of both SpaceX and Tesla, has proposed a system called the hyperloop. The system would consist of two tubes connecting cities, say San Francisco and Los Angeles. People and cargo would travel through these tubes in pods propelled by electromagnets in a low-pressure environment, with cushions of air levitating them. The pods would travel at 700 miles an hour, making transit times last minutes instead of hours.

Uber, the rideshare company, is developing a flying

for projects like the Transcontinental Railroad in the 1860s, the construction of the Panama Canal in the early twentieth century, and various dams and electrical infrastructure projects that were part of Franklin D. Roosevelt's New Deal in the 1930s. During the 1950s President Dwight D. Eisenhower used federal funds to launch the interstate highway system. And in 2009, newly elected president Barack Obama expressed support for **shovel-ready projects** as part of an package of legislation designed to stimulate the economy in the wake of a financial crisis that began in 2007.

The essays that follow in this chapter examine some of the arguments for and against the federal government's involvement in infrastructure projects.

car that could take commuters from the suburbs to urban hubs in a few minutes. Passengers would board one of these flying taxis in a suburban station and then fly to a rooftop air pad, high over rush-hour traffic, and then proceed to work by elevator and ground transport.

Self-driving cars could be hooked up to an AI-driven navigation network. With the computer driving, traffic jams could be avoided through the network. Not only could such a smart road system speed reduce commute time, it could eliminate a lot of expensive road building. If these self-driving cars are powered by electricity, the environment would benefit as well.

THE FEDERAL GOVERNMENT SHOULD INVEST HEAVILY IN NATIONAL INFRASTRUCTURE

Government support for infrastructure spending dates back to the beginning of the United States. Alexander Hamilton believed internal improvements would facilitate economic growth, and proposed a constitutional amendment that would allow the federal government to fund and build roads and canals. Presidents Thomas Jefferson and James Madison facilitated the creation of a national road from Baltimore west to the Ohio Valley, using funds from the sale of western lands to pay the states to build the road.

As the nineteenth century progressed, infrastructure spending became more mainstream. Senator Henry Clay's proposed "American System" advocated internal improvements, intergovernmental grants, and nationally directed monetary policy based upon central banking. Opposition to federal participation in internal improvements declined slowly during the nineteenth century.

"Internal improvements during the early republic were generally restricted to facilitating the transportation of the post—a federal responsibility—by improving roads, bridges, ports, waterways, tunnels, dams, and similar transportation and common-use infrastructure," explains an article from the Center for the Study of Federalism. "Later, internal improvements would include education institutions, forts and military installations, the national bank, homesteading and land policy, and by the twenty-

The Erie Canal took eight years to build. When completed in 1825, it opened the Great Lakes and Northwest Territory to trade and emigrants.

first century, internal improvements would include all areas of policy conceivably related to economic development infrastructure."[29]

As a member of Congress in the 1840s, Abraham Lincoln was a champion of infrastructure spending. In an 1848 speech, Lincoln proposed, "Let the nation take hold of the larger works, and the States the smaller ones; and thus, working in a meeting direction, discreetly, but steadily and firmly, what is made unequal in one place may be equalized in another, extravagance avoided, and the whole country put on that career of prosperity which shall correspond with its extent of territory, its natural resources, and the intelligence and enterprise of its people."[30] As president, Lincoln helped to facilitate construction of the Transcontinental Railroad, which helped to open the American West to settlement.

The meeting of the Union Pacific and Central Pacific railroad lines at Promontory Point, Utah, in 1869. The federal government provided generous financing to private companies that built the transcontinental railroad.

During the Great Depression, infrastructure spending literally saved democracy. The theory behind New Deal spending on roads, bridges, and so on was not just that these things would improve America's economy, but that the government had an obligation to provide jobs to unemployed Americans. In return, the people working to build such projects would help the United States grow itself out of economic malaise. "So in Roosevelt's America, digging a drainage ditch was not just a job, but the workers' contribution to making their community, and in turn the country, a better place," notes an article in *Popular Mechanics*. "Building a school wasn't just a way to make an income, but investing in the next generation. Damming the local river wasn't only improving one's lot in life, but also providing electricity to help one's neighbors."[31]

The engine of New Deal infrastructure spending was the Works Progress Administration. The WPA started as a jobs program, working on small local projects like roads, bridges, schools, community parks, and drainage ditches. But the WPA would eventually expand, and engage in the most extensive building program in American history. Major projects included construction of La Guardia Airport in New York or the Riverwalk in San Antonio, Texas.

"The overall numbers are staggering," notes *Popular Mechanics*. "The agency covered the U.S. with 650,000 miles of road, built 78,000 bridges, erected 125,000 civilian and military buildings, and constructed or improved 800 airports. More than infrastructure, the laborers of the

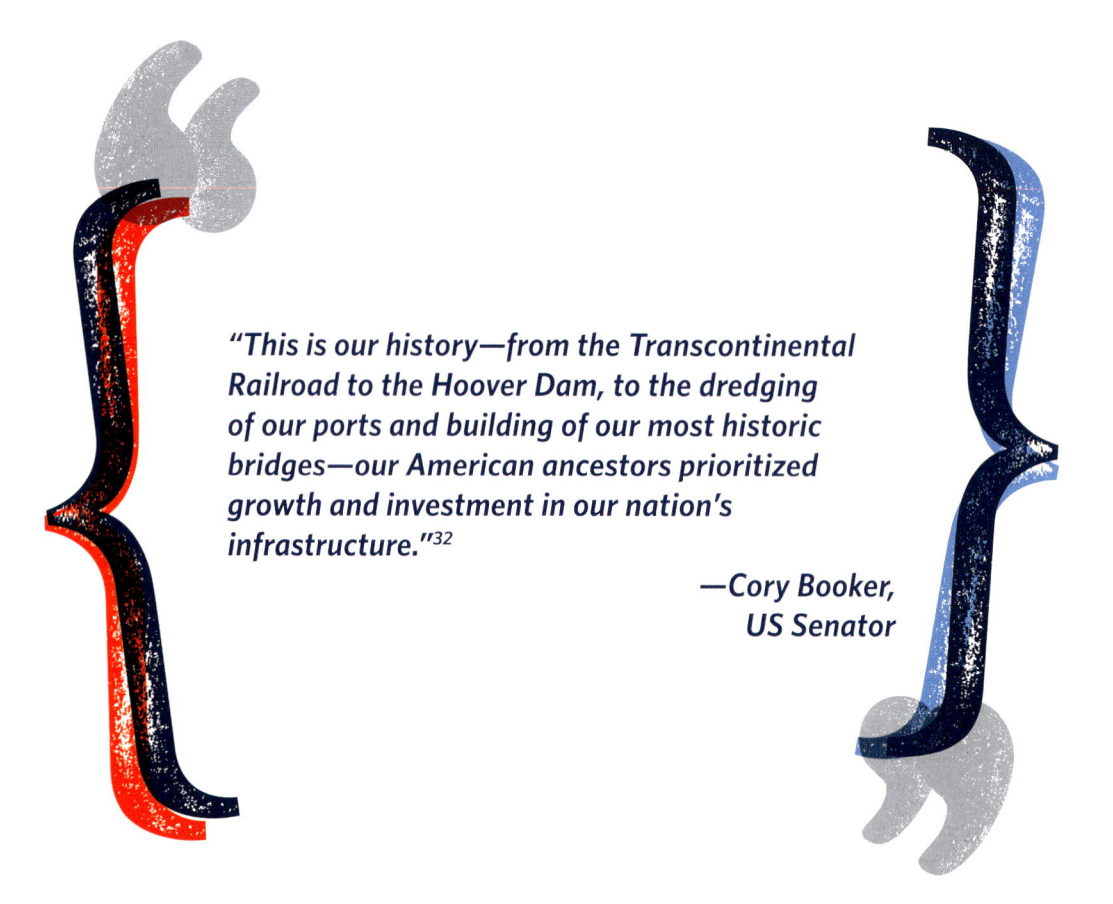

> "This is our history—from the Transcontinental Railroad to the Hoover Dam, to the dredging of our ports and building of our most historic bridges—our American ancestors prioritized growth and investment in our nation's infrastructure."[32]
>
> —Cory Booker, US Senator

WPA worked in schools, serving 900 million hot lunches to hungry children, and operated 1,500 nurseries. They also provided arts and culture, putting on 225,000 concerts, plus thousands of plays, circuses, and puppet shows. They produced nearly half a million works of art, including ones painted by Jackson Pollock. The WPA's Federal Writers' Project wrote 276 full-length books, featuring pieces from soon-to-be famous writers John Steinbeck and May Swenson."[33]

About twenty years later, President Dwight Eisenhower fought for and passed the Federal Highway Act of 1956. According to the National Highway Administration, his support for this huge infrastructure project stemmed from two experiences: one in post-World War I America, and one during World War II.

The first involved a cross-country trip in 1919 by a convoy of Army military vehicles, following the Lincoln Highway, which ran between New York City and San Francisco. The result was a disaster, with unpaved roads, weak bridges, and constant breakdowns of vehicles. The trip took sixty-two days.

As the Allied armies entered Germany during the Second World War, Eisenhower was introduced to a modern highway system, the autobahn network of four-lane superhighways. Eisenhower envisioned a similar network of interstate highways in the United States, and fought to make this dream a reality. As a result, the cross-country trip that took two months in 1919 can now be easily completed in five days.

Infrastructure spending not only improves the movement of goods and services, thus stimulating the economy, but also provides jobs and saves money in the long run.

THE FEDERAL GOVERNMENT SHOULD NOT INVEST HEAVILY IN NATIONAL INFRASTRUCTURE

There is an idea that federal spending on infrastructure helped the United States to escape from the Great Depression of the 1930s. However, as the Cato Institute points out in an analysis of New Deal, those projects did not increase the number of jobs in the economy, because they were funded using money from taxpayers—who consequently had less to spend on purchases that would have stimulated the economy, such as consumer goods or entertainment. "This is a classic case of the seen versus the unseen," noted Cato. "We can see the jobs created by New Deal spending, but we cannot see jobs destroyed by New Deal taxing."[34]

In addition, those some of the New Deal projects created a great deal of damage. For example, dams built to produce hydroelectricity under the Tennessee Valley Authority program flooded an estimated 750,000 acres. Tens of thousands of families were forced to move from their homes. Many of them were poor African-American sharecroppers, who received no compensation for the loss of their homes.

Amity Shlaes, whose critique of the New Deal, "The Forgotten Man" has caused a great deal of controversy, also takes a dim view of 1930s infrastructure spending. "Many of the jobs that the early New Deal produced were not merely temporary but also limited in economic value," writes Shlaes. "It was in these years that the political term

> "We have environmental impact studies to do, planning to consider, lawsuits to fight over the snail darter and so on. Maybe all of those are just great things for us to be doing, but they do mean that any project of any size we get started on today will actually break ground in perhaps four or five years and will be completed in perhaps a decade or more. Infrastructure just isn't a form of spending that can be done quickly these days. Therefore the effect on aggregate demand, the use of infrastructure as a form of fiscal policy, just doesn't make sense today."[35]
>
> —Tim Worstall, senior fellow, Adam Smith Institute

'boondoggle,' to describe costly make-work, was coined. It came from 'boondoggling,' the word for leather craft projects subsidized by New Deal work-relief programs.... Work-relief earnings were usually not sufficient to offset other Depression losses.

"What about spending? The Depression tells us that public works are probably less effective than improving the environment for entrepreneurs and new companies."[36]

The Foundation for Economic Education breaks down the two most common arguments in support of government spending on infrastructure. The first is

Relatively few major infrastructure projects are actually "shovel-ready." It can take years to work through environmental lawsuits before breaking ground on new construction.

that government investment spending can be used to "stimulate" the economy and put people back to work. The second is that smart, efficient investments can help enhance long-term productivity growth

"These two ambitions often conflict," notes the Foundation. "Attempts to stimulate quickly and get people back to work will likely result in sloppy project selection and the hiring of more labor than would be most efficient. And since government is, well, government, it's a pretty good bet that infrastructure funds will go preferentially to the well-connected."[37]

Another problem with government investment is that infrastructure projects can be overtaken by new and unanticipated technological improvements that come from the private sector. "The federal government spent a lot of money building and maintaining coastal lighthouses—

Private development of a high-speed transportation system, such as the "hyperloop" proposed by Elon Musk, could reduce freeway congestion in California.

Should Infrastructure Investments Be Privatized?

until GPS technology made them obsolete," notes *Reason* magazine. "Cities spent lots of money acquiring land for reservoirs and building aqueducts—but advances in desalinization and wastewater treatment technology today can make some of those earlier investments look shortsighted."[38]

While the constitutional argument against federal government infrastructure spending is not often heard, except in certain libertarian circles, some cogent objections to such projects do exist. The economic stimulus is often temporary. The projects lead to a lot of wasteful spending, corruption, and unintended consequences. A better way to create infrastructure is to create conditions for the private sector to provide such needed improvements.

TEXT-DEPENDENT QUESTIONS

1. Name some examples of infrastructure.
2. What government entity financed and built the Erie Canal?
3. What were some unintended effects of New Deal infrastructure spending?
4. Why did President Dwight Eisenhower support building the interstate highway system?

RESEARCH PROJECTS

Develop a rough design of an infrastructure project that will benefit your community. It could be a new road, bridge, an airport, or even a high-tech project such as a smart road network. Discuss the pros and cons of having the government finance and direct the project as opposed to providing incentives for the private sector to do so.

WORDS TO UNDERSTAND

repository—a place where things are stored.

research and development—the process of creating new products and services and improve old ones.

STEM—an acronym, used to describe educational classes in the fields of science, technology, engineering, and math.

vortex—a mass of whirling fluid or air.

CHAPTER 4
HOW HEAVILY SHOULD GOVERNMENT INVEST IN SCIENCE AND TECHNOLOGY RESEARCH?

At one time in US history, scientific research and the development of new technologies was mostly private. That quality called "American ingenuity" caused many inventions to pour out of American workshops, including Eli Whitney's cotton gin, Robert Fulton's steamboat, Cyrus McCormick's mechanical reaper, Thomas Edison's lightbulb, Alexander Graham Bell's telephone, and a host of other products that made people's lives easier.

The Smithsonian Institution's founding in the 1840s marked an early attempt to create a government-supported entity for the furtherance of science. Financed initially with a private endowment, the Smithsonian became a **repository** for specimens and artifacts collected by exploratory expeditions conducted by the US military. One of the early research projects conducted by the Smithsonian involved weather research.

Nevertheless, government-funded science and technology generally were conducted on an ad hoc basis, or limited to the development of military weapons and technologies before World War II. The National Advisory Council for Aeronautics (NACA) was an example. Established in 1915, NACA conducted aviation research, developing technology that helped the American military but could also be applied to civilian needs. Another was the National Institutes of Health, created in the 1870s to seeks cures and treatments for diseases.

During the Great Depression, the Roosevelt administration provided some funding for science and technology improvements in hopes of restarting the US economy. However, during World War II it became clear that science and technology were critical to victory over the Axis powers. The Manhattan Project, which created the first atomic weapons, was a major undertaking that involved tens of thousands of scientists and cost billions of dollars. The development of the B-29 bomber, which dropped tons of bombs in the Pacific Theater of the war—

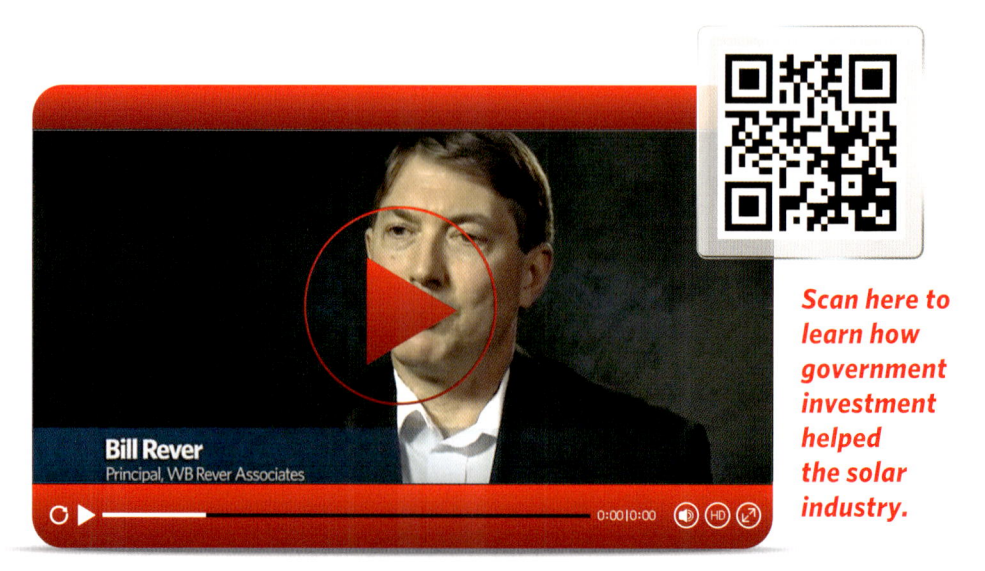

Scan here to learn how government investment helped the solar industry.

The vast scientific facility at Oak Ridge, Tennessee, one of several utilized as part of the Manhattan Project, which constructed the first atomic weapons during the Second World War.

including the atomic bombs dropped on Hiroshima and Nagasaki—also cost billions. American scientists were also able to create a process for mass-producing penicillin, a mold that was highly effective at preventing bacterial infections. This drug saved the lives of countless wounded soldiers—and since the war, has helped to prevent an estimated 200 million military and civilian deaths worldwide.

Given the success of the World War II effort, spending by the federal government on civilian **research and development** (R&D) increased dramatically during the post-war period. For example, the National Science

Foundation was created to further research and education in the non-medical sciences, such as engineering, chemistry, math, and physics.

In the late 1950s NACA evolved into the National Air and Space Administration (NASA). This agency oversaw the development of rockets, landed men on the moon, developed the space shuttle and the International Space Station, and has sent unmanned probes throughout the

NASA'S PRIVATE PARTNERSHIPS

Although the annual budget for NASA makes up less than 0.5 percent of federal spending, because NASA is a high-profile government agency its spending is under intense scrutiny. The space agency has tried to cut costs as well as establish greater links between what it does and the commercial sector.

The Commercial Orbital Transportation Systems program was undertaken in the wake of the space shuttle *Columbia* accident in 2003, to allow the International Space Station to be resupplied using commercial spacecraft. The Commercial Crew program is due to follow. Under this program, spacecraft operated by companies like SpaceX and Boeing will be responsible for taking astronauts to and from the space station. The first test flights took place in 2019.

solar system. Much of the technology that NASA developed for space exploration has applications in civilian areas: solar panels, improved rubber tires, useful software, and products like memory foam. And the data that NASA missions have collected help humans to better understand the Earth, as well as the larger universe.

The National Oceanic and Atmospheric Agency (NOAA) was formed in 1970 out of several smaller agencies. NOAA conducts research into the Earth's environment. NOAA is a crucial agency for gathering scientific data on threats to the environment, especially climate change.

The Defense Advanced Research Projects Agency

More recently, NASA selected nine companies to develop lunar landers for a proposed effort to return to the moon by the mid-2020s. Robotic probes would be sent to the moon on commercial landers, with NASA buying space on them to carry instruments and other payloads. When Americans return to the moon, it will be on commercial spacecraft, not government craft like the Apollo program of the 1960s.

These programs are not only designed to save NASA money, but also to address the government vs. private spending argument on science and technology. The government provides most or all of the money, but the private sector provides the solutions. Spacecraft and technologies developed under these commercial partnerships can be used for private-sector purposes.

(DARPA) was formed in 1958 as part of the US Department of Defense. DARPA conducts research and development related to technology with military applications, although its projects often have civilian uses as well. Most famously, in the late 1960s the agency developed ARPANET, the predecessor of the modern-day internet.

The question of whether or not the United States should fund science and technology has largely been settled, except in some libertarian circles. The big question, however, is how much and where the government should conduct investments in the **STEM** (science, technology, engineering, and math) fields.

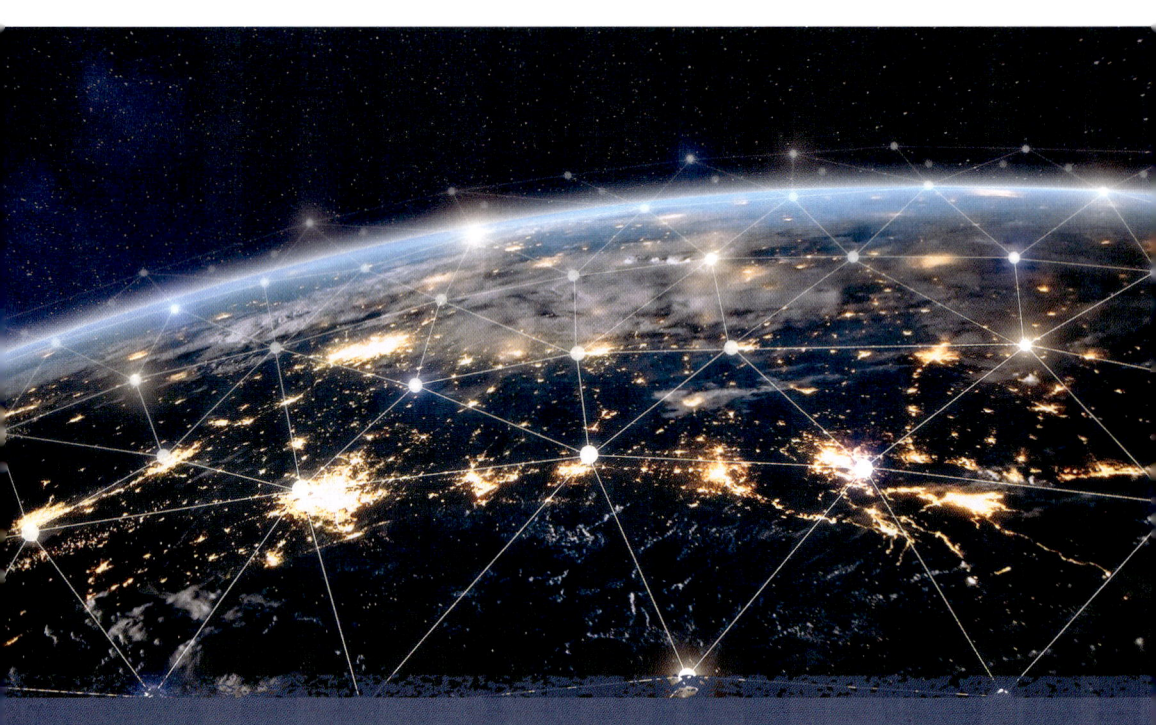

Government-funded research made the internet and other technologies that people take for granted today possible.

GOVERNMENT INVESTMENT IN SCIENCE AND TECHNOLOGY CAN CREATE JOBS

The United States is the world's leading economy and one of its wealthiest nations per capita today largely because it has always invested in innovation. The US spends more than any other country on research and development. According to the work of economists like the Nobel Prize-winner Robert Solow and others, this spending has made American richer.

"Exponential economic growth such as we have experienced comes from positive feedback, where the production of something enables you to produce even more," write William Press and Hunter Rawlings in the *Huffington Post*. "Economists note that only capital—including human, intellectual, and environmental capita—can fuel exponential growth. Solow and subsequent researchers found that at most half of historical growth could be attributed to known factors. The unexplained part, sometimes estimated to be as large as 85 percent of growth, was termed the 'Solow residual.' Subsequent work showed that the bulk of that residual could be explained by positing a new factor in production: technological progress."[39]

Press, a professor of computer science and integrative biology at the University of Texas at Austin, and Rawlings, the president of the Association of American Universities, contend in their essay that public spending on science and technology produces wealth. Furthermore, they argue that *only* public spending can provide the full effect. "Technology produces wealth, and it produces more technological progress, which produces even more growth, thus enabling a virtuous cycle of exponential growth," they write. "Technological progress depends on basic research; this is why economists have found that investments in basic research can produce returns between 20 percent and 60 percent per year....Basic research leading to scientific discovery is, therefore, a public good."[40]

In 2014, Congress asked the National Academy of Sciences to assess the economic return on government investment in research. The Academy's report *Furthering America's Research Enterprise* explains why it's hard to directly measure and manipulate the economic benefits of government-funded research, and concludes that the government should focus on cultivating a world-class basic research community, and the economic returns will come. "Most of the metrics aimed at capturing the commercial value of federally funded research are misleading, and attempts to directly boost economic returns—such as urging universities to patent their scientists' discoveries— tend to have unintended consequences that make these policies self-defeating," notes the report. "The best way to get the most out of our research is to help researchers in government, academia, and industry do what they naturally want to do."[41]

NASA is often touted as a special case where it comes to debating the economic effects of research and

In the United States, agencies like the Centers for Disease Control and Prevention are responsible for protecting communities from disease epidemics and other health threats to public health.

How Heavily Should Government Invest in Science and Technology Research?

development. In the mid-1970s, Chase Econometrics evaluated the economic benefits of Apollo-era NASA research and development. The results were illuminating:

> NASA R & D spending increases the rate of technological change and reduces the rate of inflation for two reasons. First, in the short run, it redistributes demand in the direction of the high-technology industries, thus improving aggregate productivity in the economy. As a result, NASA R & D spending tends to be more stabilizing in a recovery period than general government spending.
>
> Second, in the long run, it expands the production possibility frontier of the economy by increasing the rate of technological progress. This improves labor productivity further, which results in lower labor costs and hence lower prices. A slower rate of inflation leads in turn to a more rapid rise in real disposable income, permitting consumers to purchase the additional goods and services being produced and generating greater employment.[42]

Moreover, the Chase Econometric Study suggested that increasing NASA funding would have a corresponding increase in economic benefits.

NASA space technology is often repurposed in areas beyond the original application for space exploration. In a column in *Discover Magazine*, Phil Plait offered an example derived from the testing of a new rocket engine. The engine was designed so that fuel would spin into an engine chamber before igniting to create a **vortex**. This focused the fuel flow, keeping it closer to the center of the chamber, so that when the fuel ignited the walls of the chamber did not heat up. The innovative rocket technology was subsequently adapted to create a way to pump water more quickly and efficiently for fighting fires.

"This new system put out a fire more quickly, using less water, and—critically—with fewer firefighters needed to operate the hose," wrote Plait. "This frees up needed firefighters to do other important tasks on the job, and therefore makes fighting fires faster and safer. There is no way you could've predicted beforehand that investing in NASA would have led to the creation of this specific innovation in life-saving technology. But it's a rock-solid guarantee that investing in science always leads to innovations that have far-ranging and critical benefits to our lives."[43]

> "Once you have an innovation culture, even those who are not scientists or engineers—poets, actors, journalists—they, as communities, embrace the meaning of what it is to be scientifically literate. They embrace the concept of an innovation culture. They vote in ways that promote it. They don't fight science, and they don't fight technology."[44]
>
> —Neil deGrasse Tyson, American astrophysicist

Government spending on science and technology derives economic benefits because research and development thus enabled create new products and new processes that prove useful for private business. Some of the ways research and development does this are difficult to predict beforehand, but nevertheless, it happens.

While it may be hard to draw a direct line between basic science research and economic benefits, most experts agree that such a connection exists.

GOVERNMENT INVESTMENT IN SCIENCE AND TECHNOLOGY DOESN'T STIMULATE THE ECONOMY

Matt Ridley, a British journalist and businessman, suggests that government-funded science research has little or no effect on the economy, at least compared to privately funded R&D. He wrote in the *Wall Street Journal*:

> In 2003, the Organization for Economic Cooperation and Development published a paper on the "sources of economic growth in OECD countries" between 1971 and 1998 and found, to its surprise, that whereas privately funded research and development stimulated economic growth, publicly funded research had no economic impact whatsoever. None. This earthshaking result has never been challenged or debunked. It is so inconvenient to the argument that science needs public funding that it is ignored.[45]

Moreover, advocates of government spending on science have things completely backwards, writes Ridley:

> When you examine the history of innovation you find, again and again, that scientific breakthroughs are the effect, not the cause, of technological change. It is no accident that astronomy blossomed in the wake of the age of exploration. The steam engine owed almost nothing to the science of thermodynamics, but the science of thermodynamics owed almost everything to the steam engine. The discovery of the structure of DNA depended heavily on X-ray crystallography of biological molecules, a technique developed in the wool industry to try to improve textiles.[46]

Indeed, the idea that government funding of science drives innovation and thus economic growth is not only wrong, but such funding is counterproductive. Government research spending is less effective than private spending, because the science tends to follow the innovation.

It is in the best interest of corporations like the pharmaceutical giant Eli Lilly and Co. to fund scientific research and development, in order to create products that their customers need.

The practical tinkerers find something, then science is employed to work out why what they've found works.

Major companies and private foundations can afford to do research and development. For example, the John D. Rockefeller Foundation funded both the discovery of DNA and the development of penicillin—two of the most important discoveries of the twentieth century. More recently, the Bill and Melinda Gates Foundation has devoted more than $40 billion to research on malaria and other infectious diseases in the developing world. The Howard Hughes Medical Institute has spent over $700 million on biomedical research and science education, while the Michael J. Fox Foundation has contributed a similar amount toward understanding Parkinson's disease.

A problem with government funding of science is that it is often wasteful, with millions of dollars spent on esoteric research programs each year. Former US Senator William Proxmire, a Democrat from Wisconsin, was famous for awarding the "Golden Fleece Award" to research grants that he considered to be examples of government waste. Programs that attracted his anger included a 1975 National Science Foundation grant of $84,000 to study why people fall in love, as well as programs funded by

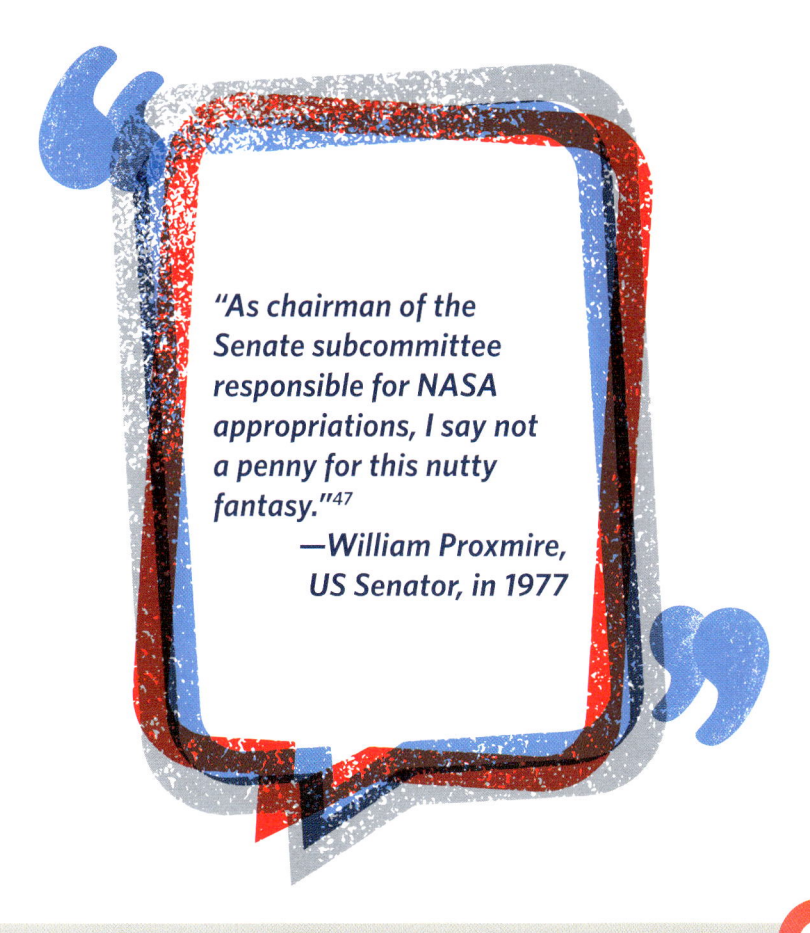

> "As chairman of the Senate subcommittee responsible for NASA appropriations, I say not a penny for this nutty fantasy."[47]
> —William Proxmire, US Senator, in 1977

NASA and the Office of Naval Research. In 1979, Proxmire awarded the Golden Fleece to the NASA program Search for Extraterrestrial Intelligence (SETI). Congress eventually canceled NASA funding for SETI, but the program has been kept alive with private funding.

Another issue is that spending on NASA programs take money away from other priorities, particularly social spending. During the 1960s, newspapers in the African American community opposed the use of taxpayer funds for space research at a time when many black families were struggling at the margins of the working class. An editorial in the *Los Angeles Sentinel*, for example, argued against the Apollo program, saying, "It would appear that the fathers of our nation would allow a few thousand hungry people to die for the lack of a few thousand dollars while they would contaminate the moon and its sterility for the sake of 'progress' and spend billions of dollars in the process, while people are hungry, ill-clothed, poorly educated (if at all)."[48] Similarly, the Trump administration's proposal to send more scientists to the moon by 2024 through the Artemis program draws funding away from social programs and issues that many Americans believe should be a higher priority, such as education, repairing the nation's crumbling infrastructure, immigration reform, and social justice for minorities.

Ultimately, government spending on science should be reduced because it does not help the economy in a measurable way.

TEXT-DEPENDENT QUESTIONS

1. What is the purpose of the National Science Foundation?
2. What was Senator Proxmire's objection to government-funded science?
3. What did Chase Econometrics conclude about NASA research and development spending?

RESEARCH PROJECTS

Develop a grant proposal for a science research project. The project can concern anything from health to applied physics. Justify the project for its possible real-world benefits as well as for the knowledge that may be derived from the results.

WORDS TO UNDERSTAND

regulation—a rule or a directive made by the government to control how a thing is done or how people behave.

deregulation—the reduction or removal of government regulations, especially in the economic sphere.

monopoly—a company or other entity that has sole control over a product or a number of products.

CHAPTER 5

DOES DEREGULATION HELP OR HURT WORKERS AND THE ECONOMY?

United States government **regulation** of the private sector began in the late nineteenth century, in response to the perceived abuses of big business, especially in the formation of monopolies. The 1887 Interstate Commerce Act created the first independent regulatory commission. The five-member Interstate Commerce Commission's first responsibility was to ensure that businesses engaged in interstate commerce, such as railroads, charged fair rates. Later legislation broadened the ICC's responsibilities to include worker safety and anti-discrimination.

Another noteworthy piece of legislation that regulated businesses was the Sherman Anti-Trust Act of 1890. The purpose was to break up large corporations that held a **monopoly** in their industry. The goal was to promote competition, which would make prices more fair for consumers. During Theodore Roosevelt's presidency the Sherman Anti-Trust Act was strengthened, revised, and put to thorough use.

Additional business regulation was adopted by Congress during the presidency of Woodrow Wilson from 1912 until 1920. In 1914, the Clayton Anti-Trust Act prohibited discrimination in prices among purchasers, exclusive deals tying a purchaser to a single supplier, and any action that "substantially lessens competition or tends to create a monopoly." At this time, the Federal Trade Commission was created to "prevent the unlawful suppression of competition."[49]

In addition to the trade commission, dozens of other laws throughout the decades have been enacted to regulate business. The Meat Inspection Act of 1906, the Securities and Exchange Act of 1934, the Truth in Packaging Act of 1966, and the Consumer Credit Protection Act of 1969, all serve to protect individuals from unfair

To learn more about deregulation and its economic effects, scan here.

practices perpetrated by business greed. These landmark pieces of legislation provided a precedent for the federal government to punish any business that stifles competition or acts unfairly toward individuals.

In the 1970s, President Richard Nixon created two more important regulatory agencies: the Environmental

The 1978 Airline Deregulation Act eliminated federal government control over certain aspects of the air transportation industry. The Federal Aviation Administration still maintains strict safety regulations. However, since deregulation the number of available flights has increased while fares have gotten lower.

Protection Agency (EPA) and the Occupational Safety and Health Administration (OSHA). Since then, however, the trend in Washington has been toward reducing or eliminating government regulations. President Jimmy Carter started the drive by **deregulating** transportation

RIDE-SHARING IN AUSTIN, TEXAS

With federal, state, and local governments all imposing regulations on businesses, it is only to be expected that some conflicts would arise. One recent conflict was over the regulation of ridesharing services such as Uber and Lyft. In 2016, the city of Austin, Texas, passed an ordinance requiring ridesharing drivers to be fingerprinted. When two of the major ridesharing companies, Uber and Lyft, were unable to have the ordinance overturned, they ended service in Austin in May 2016.

The conflict came to the Texas Legislature's attention. Lawmakers were concerned that Texas would have a patchwork of different regulations affecting ridesharing. The Texas state government was also more business-friendly that the relatively liberal Austin city government. After some negotiation between lawmakers and ridesharing company lobbyists, the legislature passed a state-wide measure industries, including airlines, railroads, and trucking firms. Subsequent presidents championed energy, environmental, telecommunication, and banking deregulation.

American government agencies remain empowered to write regulations on businesses and industries. But how much regulation is enough, and when do the rules start to impede private business activity and affect the economy? The following essays will examine both sides of that critical question.

regulating ridesharing that was signed into law in May 2017. According to the *Texas Tribune*:

"House Bill 100 undoes local rules that the two companies have argued are overly burdensome for their business models. It requires ride-hailing companies to have a permit from the Texas Department of Licensing and Regulation and pay an annual fee of $5,000 to operate throughout the state. It also calls for companies to perform local, state, and national criminal background checks on drivers annually—but doesn't require drivers to be fingerprinted."[50]

As a result of the uniform regulation, ride sharing flourishes in Texas, providing people with a viable alternative for transportation that is cheaper than a taxi and more efficient and flexible than mass transit. The story illustrates how regulations can sometimes reach a happy medium of encouraging rather than impeding a new industry, albeit through a messy political process.

DEREGULATION WILL LEAD TO ECONOMIC GROWTH AND JOB CREATION

Government regulations are like hidden taxes, which increase prices for consumers. They also protect established firms from competition, by creating barriers that make it harder for new companies to enter a particular industry. Suppressing competition like this also suppresses innovation. As one analysis notes, "[regulatory] costs will tend to exceed their benefits unless subjected to rigorous cost-benefit analysis and a thorough vetting process."[51]

Removing regulations and allowing the free market to regulate itself is a much more effective approach. In *The Wealth of Nations*, Adam Smith argued that an economy will function best when the government leaves people alone to by and sell among themselves. Smith suggested that in a free market, self-interested traders would compete with each other and fair prices would set themselves naturally. Whenever enough people demand a particular product or service, new businesses will enter the market to supply it. Smith called this balancing force the free market's "invisible hand."

Where there are no government regulations on the market, customers will purchase from the business that charges the lowest price. To compete, other businesses must either lower prices or offer something better than their competitors. This benefits consumers, who wind up getting better goods at a fair price.

"A better approach is certainly to permit the automatic

> "State interference in economic life, which calls itself economic policy, has done nothing but destroy economic life. Prohibitions and regulations have by their general obstructive tendency fostered the growth of the spirit of wastefulness."[52]
>
> —Ludwig Von Mises, Austrian economist

and self-regulating 'invisible hand' of the market to "manage" the production and distribution of goods and services. Price signals, competition, and the profit and loss mechanism, together revealing the underlying conditions of supply and demand, are a far more sophisticated and responsive system of accountability than the often clumsy and crony 'visible hand' of government regulation."[53]

In 2016, the Brookings Institute looked back at the effects of deregulation since the 1970s. "In virtually every deregulated industry, there have been substantial gains in efficiency," noted their report. "The firms supplying the service—new entrants and incumbents alike—produce it at costs about 30 percent lower than would have been incurred under the old regulatory regime. In addition, service quality tends to improve. Deregulation reduced airline fares, trucking costs, and railroad transportation costs by about $35 billion per year, largely through improvements in efficiency. Similarly, reductions in long-distance telephone rates came about because of improved efficiency and the FCC's more efficient pricing of interstate carrier access, not from reduced telephone company profits."[54]

After taking office in January 2017, President Donald Trump embarked on a massive deregulatory effort. By 2019, the Trump administration had 514 deregulatory measures in process, addressing issues as diverse as federal student loans and climate change. An article published in

Nobel Prize-winning economist Milton S. Friedman was a champion of free markets. He called for deregulation of industries and a reduced role for government in economic activities.

Investor's Business Daily found that taxpayers would save $8.1 billion in reduced federal regulatory costs. In addition, the Trump administration has prevented some regulations from going into effect, translating into even greater savings. "There are literally hundreds of pending rules and regulations, all with varying costs, and Trump has quietly stymied many of them," noted the *Investors Business Daily* report. "All told, 1,579 planned regulatory actions have been either withdrawn or delayed in the last year…. Trump says he wants to return to the 1960 level of regulation. That might be hard, and even require changes in law from Congress. But if he got even close to the 1960 level, the economy would surge."[55]

State and local governments also regulate businesses. California, for example, is considered to be a state with heavy regulations, as well as high taxes. Texas, on the other hand, has light regulation and low-taxes. The states are the two most populous of the United States, but their economies perform very differently. Even though California has many natural advantages over Texas, the Texas economy is growing at a much faster rate than that of California. In 2017, the most recent year for which data is available, the Texas gross domestic product grew at a rate of nearly 4 percent, while California's GDP grew only 0.1 percent. How can this be?

"So what is the explanation for the disconnect between natural advantages in California and lack of growth?" asks syndicated columnist Michael Reagan. "Easy. 120 state legislators and one moony governor are enough to single-handedly nullify all of the state's natural advantages." Reagan continued:

> Just think about it. Mining in Texas contributed over 2 percent to GDP growth. It would never happen in California. Mining means digging, and disrupting the dirt might startle a bug, and environmentalists would never sit still for that! Number two in growth production for Texas was manufacturing.
>
> That's all well and good if all you care about is jobs and economic security. But in California they care about the environment, and if workers have to be sacrificed on the altar of carbon denial, then so be it.
>
> And in California this whole idea of "growth" makes our rulers uncomfortable. It might produce carbon or encourage someone to buy a car or even worse, build a car.
>
> A political elite that disdains progress and growth is going to retard the economy in any state, regardless of natural advantages. Which is why Texas is leading California. It may have second-class weather, but it boasts first-class political leadership."[56]

Historian and Hoover Institute fellow Victor Davis Hanson has a similarly stark assessment of California, a state where he resides. "Nowhere is this paradox truer than in California, a dysfunctional natural paradise in which a group of coastal and governing magnificos virtue-signal from the world's most exclusive and beautiful enclaves," Hanson writes. "The state is currently experiencing another perfect storm of increased crime, decreased incarceration, still ongoing illegal immigration, and record poverty. All that is energized by a strapped middle class that is still fleeing the overregulated and overtaxed state, while the arriving poor take their places in hopes

Companies are more likely to invest in communities that do not impose many costly restrictions on their activities. This creates jobs and brings other economic benefits to those communities.

of generous entitlements, jobs servicing the elite, and government employment."[57]

Excessive regulations tend to stifle economic growth and job creation by increasing the burden of running a business. By contrast, light regulation spurs economic growth and the creation of jobs. The trick is to have a government that understands how business works and that does not regard business as the enemy.

REGULATIONS ARE NEEDED TO PROMOTE FAIRNESS AND TRANSPARENCY

The first government regulations of business were undertaken in the late nineteenth century in response to excesses committed by the private sector, especially in relation to creating monopolies. President Teddy Roosevelt, who earned the moniker of "the trust buster" was enthusiastic about bringing big business to heel. As UVA's Miller Center stated:

> The President also changed the government's relationship to big business. Prior to his presidency, the government had generally given the titans of industry carte blanche to accomplish their goals. Roosevelt believed that the government had the right and the responsibility to regulate big business so that its actions did not negatively affect the general public. However, he never fundamentally challenged the status of big business, believing that its existence marked a naturally occurring phase of the country's economic evolution."[58]

The last sentence is the key. Government regulation, properly understood, is not meant to destroy capitalism, but rather to bring about fairness and transparency to the private sector.

The Pew Research Center suggests that the cost of government regulations is often overestimated and their benefits ignored. "Regulatory requirements to protect the environment, workers, and consumers often lead to innovation, increased productivity, and new businesses and jobs," notes a Pew analysis. "Although an argument is sometimes made that the cost of complying with regulations is too high, that the societal benefits do

Regulations that protect the environment, ensuring clean air and water, can actually benefit the economy as well by reducing health care costs and improving worker productivity.

not justify the investment, or that job losses will result, a review of past regulations reveals just the opposite. Historically, compliance costs have been less and benefits greater than industry predictions, and regulation typically poses little challenge to economic competitiveness."[59]

For example, it cost coal-fired power plants about $20 billion to retrofit their facilities to comply with the EPA's clean air regulations. However, an EPA report found that people living in those areas made fewer visits to hospital emergency rooms, there was a lower rate of premature deaths, and that the number of workdays lost to illness was reduced as well. The EPA valued these costs at between $118 billion and $177 billion annually

Auto safety regulations have had enormous benefits as well. Seat belts and air bags have saved hundreds of thousands of lives and have decreased medical costs and auto insurance premiums.

Business leaders often complain about the cost of complying with regulations in both time and money. However, the businesses can blame themselves for cutting corners in their efforts to maximize profits, at the expense of consumers and the American public. "Over the past decades, particularly leading up to the Global Financial Crisis that unfolded from 2007-2011, too many publicly traded corporations have misstated earnings to maintain or boost the market price of their stock," notes an analysis by Investopedia. "They've violated immigration laws by hiring undocumented workers. They've broken environmental laws by illegally dumping wastes or emitting pollutants into the atmosphere or into rivers and lakes. So clearly the "no rules" approach has a cost for the general public—which is why our elected bodies are in charge of regulation in the first place. In response to some of the behaviors mentioned above, we now have entities and regulations to discourage repeats and businesses complain about them endlessly."[60]

If business could regulate itself, the government would not have to step in. However, in the real world, many businesses have not been able to stop themselves from

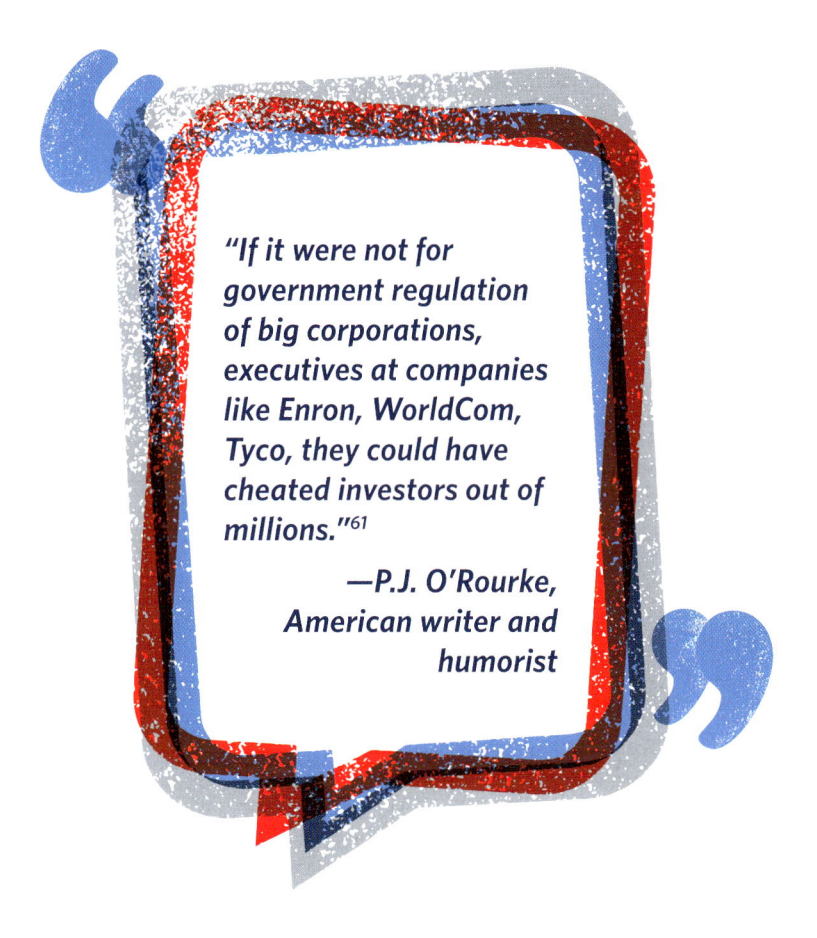

> "If it were not for government regulation of big corporations, executives at companies like Enron, WorldCom, Tyco, they could have cheated investors out of millions."[61]
>
> —P.J. O'Rourke, American writer and humorist

playing fast and loose, so government must define the rules and enforce them.

Regulations, by providing a set of clearly understandable rules, can actually help the formation of new industries. Commercial space is a prime example. Ten or twenty years ago, the idea of a vibrant commercial space sector that was not an arm of NASA and the military was considered a fantasy. Now, with the advent of such companies as SpaceX, Blue Origin, and Moon Express, the United States government has recognized the necessity of a well-designed regulatory regime. Recently President Trump signed Space Policy Directive-2, which is meant to establish a regulatory framework for commercial space. According to the industry newsletter *Space News*, industry groups welcomed the policy's signing.

"We've been innovating here at home and competing around the world under the burden of regulations written decades ago, in some cases rooted in the Cold War," said Alan Stern, chairman of the board of the Commercial Spaceflight Federation, in a statement. "Now we can foresee a more streamlined legal and administrative regime that will allow us to continue to help transform how Americans access and use space."[62]

No one wants a "wild west" situation in space. Regulations are needed for commercial space businesses to comply with international laws, including the Outer Space Treaty, which was written over fifty years ago, before a commercial space sector was even contemplated.

Government regulation has many benefits. Regulations provide a check on business and prevent business from committing excesses that harm customers and the economy. They provide numerous benefits that are often underestimated and exceed the costs of compliance. Government regulations are necessary because historically, business cannot regulate itself. Business often welcomes regulations because they provide a set of easily understood rules that foster economic growth, job creation, and competitiveness.

TEXT-DEPENDENT QUESTIONS

1. What was the first law requiring the regulation of private commerce called, and what agency did it create?
2. Which two regulatory agencies did President Richard Nixon create?
3. Which president oversaw the deregulation of the airline and railroad industries?

RESEARCH PROJECTS

Imagine that a new industry has arisen that builds robot servants capable of doing anything for its owner that a human being would be able to do. Develop a set of regulations for this new industry, justifying them on the basis of obeying federal law, principles of fairness, and other benefits.

SERIES GLOSSARY OF KEY TERMS

affidavit—a sworn statement, in writing, that sets out a person's testimony.

affirmative action programs—programs that are intended to improve the educational or employment opportunities of members of minority groups and women.

BCE and CE—alternatives to the traditional Western designation of calendar eras, which used the birth of Jesus as a dividing line. BCE stands for "Before the Common Era," and is equivalent to BC ("Before Christ"). Dates labeled CE, or "Common Era," are equivalent to Anno Domini (AD, or "the Year of Our Lord").

colony—a country or region ruled by another country.

democracy—a country in which the people can vote to choose those who govern them.

discrimination—prejudiced outlook, action, or treatment, often in a negative way.

detention center—a place where people claiming asylum and refugee status are held while their case is investigated.

ethnic cleansing—an attempt to rid a country or region of a particular ethnic group. The term was first used to describe the attempt by Serb nationalists to rid Bosnia of Muslims.

felony—a serious crime; in the United States, a felony is any crime for which the punishment is more than one year in prison or the death penalty.

fundamentalist—beliefs based on a strict biblical or scriptural interpretation of religious law.

median—In statistics, the number that falls in the center of a group, meaning half the numbers are higher than the number and half are lower.

minority—a part of a population different from the majority in some characteristics and often subjected to differential treatment.

paranoia—a mental disorder characterized by the strong belief that the person is being unfairly persecuted.

parole—releasing someone sentenced to prison before the full sentence is served, granted for good behavior.

plaintiff—a person making a complaint in a legal case in civil court.

pro bono—a Latin phrase meaning "for the public good," referring to legal work undertaken without payment or at a reduced fee as a public service.

racial profiling—projecting the characteristics of a few people onto the entire population of a group; for example, when police officers stop people on suspicion of criminal activity solely because of their race.

racism—discrimination against a particular group of people based solely on their racial background.

segregation—the separation or isolation of a race, class, or group from others in society. This can include restricting areas in which members of the race, class, or group can live; placing barriers to social interaction; separate educational facilities; or other discriminatory means.

ORGANIZATIONS TO CONTACT

American Association for the
Advancement of Science
1200 New York Avenue NW
Washington, DC 20005
Phone: (202) 326-6400
Website: https://www.aaas.org/programs/center-science-policy-and-society

American Economic Association
2014 Broadway, Suite 305
Nashville, TN 37203
Phone: (615) 322-2595
Website: www.aeaweb.org

Council of Economic Advisers
1800 G Street NW
Washington, DC 20502
Phone: (202) 395-5084.
Website: www.whitehouse.gov/cea

National Institutes of Health
9000 Rockville Pike
Bethesda, Maryland 20892
Phone: (301) 496-4000
Website: https://www.nih.gov

US Department of Commerce
1401 Constitution Avenue NW
Washington, DC 20230
Phone: (202) 482-2000
Email: TheSec@doc.gov
Website: www.usa.gov/federal-agencies/u-s-department-of-commerce

US Department of Health
and Human Services
330 C. Street, SW
Washington, DC 20201
Website: https://www.acf.hhs.gov/ohs

US Department of Labor
200 Constitution Avenue NW
Washington, DC 20210
Phone: (866) 487-236
Website: www.dol.gov

University of Chicago
Department of Economics
1126 E. 59th Street
Chicago, Illinois 60637
Phone: (773) 702-5079
Email: economics@uchicago.edu
Website: https://economics.uchicago.edu

FURTHER READING / INTERNET RESOURCES

FURTHER READING

Ball, Laurence M. *The Fed and Lehman Brothers: Setting the Record Straight on a Financial Disaster*. New York: Cambridge University Press, 2018.

Edelman, Peter. *So Rich, So Poor: Why It's So Hard to End Poverty in America*. New York: The New Press, 2013.

Ebenstein, Lanny. *Milton Friedman*. New York: Palgrave Macmillan, 2007.

Mazzucato, Mariana. *The Entrepreneurial State: Debunking Public vs. Private Sector Myths*. New York: Public Affairs, 2015.

Tirado, Linda. *Hand to Mouth: Living in Bootstrap America*. New York: Penguin Random House, 2015.

FURTHER READING

https://www.heritage.org/economic-and-property-rights
The Heritage Foundation is a conservative think tank that tends to take a free market view on economic issues.

https://www.brookings.edu/about-economic-studies
The Brookings Institute is a left-of-center think tank that offers a mix of free market and government solutions to economic problems.

https://www.cato.org/research/economic-theory
The Cato Institute is a libertarian think tank that hews toward private solutions to economic questions.

https://www.nasa.gov/offices/education/about/index.html
NASA provides a wealth of information on space, science, and technology subjects related to its mission.

https://www.nsf.gov/publications
The National Science Foundation's document library provides numerous materials about the scientific programs that it supports.

https://www.transportation.gov
The US Department of Transportation provides a wealth of information concerning infrastructure on its web site.

CHAPTER NOTES

[1] Adam Smith, *The Wealth Of Nations* (1776). Available at the Adam Smith Institute (accessed April 2019). https://www.adamsmith.org/adam-smith-quotes/

[2] "Milton Friedman in his own words," *The Wall Street Journal* (November 16, 2006). https:// www.wsj.com/articles/SB116369649781325207

[3] Karl Marx and Friedrich Engels, *The Communist Manifesto* (1848). Available at Marxists.org (accessed April 2019). https:// www.marxists.org/archive/marx/works/1848/communist-manifesto/ch02.htm

[4] Bernie Sanders, quoted in Tessa Stuart, "What's a Democratic Socialist? Bernie Sanders Explains," *Rolling Stone* (November 15, 2015). https:// www.rollingstone.com/politics/politics-news/whats-a-democratic-socialist-bernie-sanders-explains-63649/

[5] The Eleanor Roosevelt Papers Project, "The Progressive Era (1890—1920)," George Washington University. https://www2.gwu.edu/~erpapers/teachinger/glossary/progressive-era.cfm

[6] The History Channel, "New Deal." https://www.history.com/topics/great-depression/new-deal

[7] The History Channel, "The Great Society." https://www.history.com/topics/1960s/great-society

[8] The Heritage Foundation, "2018 Index of Economic Freedom." https://www.heritage.org/index/country/hongkong

[9] John F. Kennedy, "Address to the Economic Club of New York," American Rhetoric. https:// www.americanrhetoric.com/speeches/jfkeconomicclubaddress.html

[10] Investopedia, "Tax Reform Act of 1986." https://www.investopedia.com/terms/t/taxreformac- t1986.asp

[11] Sidney Kess, "First Look at The Tax Cuts and Jobs Act of 2017," *The CPA Journal* (January 2018). https://www.cpajournal.com/2018/01/22/first-look-tax-cuts-jobs-act-2017/

[12] Murray Weidenbaum, "Regulatory Process Reform From Ford to Clinton," The Cato Institute. https://object.cato.org/sites/cato.org/files/serials/files/regulation/1991/1/reg20n1a.html

[13] Benjamin Franklin, 1789 letter, quoted in "Benjamin Franklin's Last Great Quote and the Constitution," Constitution Daily blog, National Constitution Center (November 13, 2018). https:// constitutioncenter.org/blog/benjamin-franklins-last-great-quote-and-the-constitution/

[14] Will Rogers, quoted in Edwin Feulner, "Counterpoint: Dueling with the Death

CHAPTER NOTES

Tax," The Heritage Foundation (June 9, 2017). https://www.heritage.org/taxes/commentary/counterpoint-duel- ing-the-death-tax

[15] Julia Kagan, "Federal Income Tax," Investopedia (June 23, 2017). https://www.investopedia.com/ terms/f/federal_income_tax.asp

[16] David Boaz, "One Bad and Eight Good Reasons to Cut Taxes," The Cato Institute (February 28, 2001). Cato Institute, https://www.cato.org/publications/commentary/one-bad-eight-good- reasons-cut-taxes

[17] Andrew Foy and Brenton Stransky, "Lying About Bush's Tax Cuts," *The American Thinker* (March 5, 2010). https://www.americanthinker.com/articles/2010/03/lying_about_bushs_tax_cuts.html

[18] Ronald Reagan, quoted in Jared Powers, "Nine Reagan Quotes About Taxes," House Republicans (April 24, 2015). https:// www.gop.gov/9-ronald-reagan-quotes-about-taxes/

[19] Ronald Reagan Presidential Foundation and Institute, "The Second American Revolution: Reaganomics," (accessed April 2019). https://www.reaganfoundation.org/ronald-reagan/the-presidency/economic-policy/

[20] Daniel Mitchell, "Lessons from the Reagan Tax Cuts," The Cato Institute (May 1, 2017). https://www.cato.org/blog/lessons-reagan-tax-cuts

[21] Daniel Mitchel, "Flat Tax is the Way of the Future," The Heritage Foundation (March 20, 2006). https://www.heritage.org/taxes/commentary/flat-tax-the-way-the-future

[22] Diana Furchtgott-Roth, "Six Lessons from JFK on Tax Policy," *Market Watch* (November 22, 2013). https://www.marketwatch.com/story/6-lessons-from-jfk-on-tax-policy-2013-11-22

[23] Tim Harris, "Bernie Sanders: After Tax Breaks for Billionaires, Republicans will Cut Social Security," RealClearPolitics (December 15, 2017). https://www.realclearpolitics.com/video/2017/12/15/ bernie_sanders_after_tax_breaks_for_billionaires_republicans_will_cut_social_security.html

[24] Warren Buffett, quoted in Juliann Neher, "Warren Buffett Tells ABC Rich People Should Pay Higher Taxes," Bloomberg News (November 21, 2010). https://www.bloomberg.com/news/articles/2010-11-21/warren-buffett-tells-abc-rich-people-should-pay-more-in-taxes

[25] Alan Auerbach and William Gale, "The Case Against Tax Cuts," The Brookings Institute (March 1, 1999). https://www.brookings.edu/research/the-case-against-tax-cuts/

[26] David Wessel, "What We Learned From Reagan's Tax Cuts," The Brookings Institute (December 8, 2017). https:// www.brookings.edu/blog/up-front/2017/12/08/what-we-learned-from-reagans-tax-cuts/

[27] Michael Mazerof, "Kansas Provides Compelling Evidence of Failure of 'Supply-Side' Tax Cuts," Center on Budget and Policy Priorities (January 22, 2018). https://www.cbpp.org/re- search/state-budget-and-tax/kansas-provides-compelling-evidence-of-failure-of-supply-side-tax-cuts

[28] American History, "Internal Improvements," (accessed April 2019). https://www.americanhistoryusa.com/topic/ internal-improvements/

[29] Center for the Study of Federalism, "Internal Improvements," (accessed April 2019). http://encyclopedia.federalism.org/ index.php/Internal_Improvements

[30] Abraham Lincoln, "Speech on Internal Improvements," (June 20, 1848). Discerning History (accessed April 2019). http://discern- inghistory.com/causes/3economics/lincolns-speech-on-internal-improvements/

[31] Matt Blitz, "When America's Infrastructure Saved Democracy," *Popular Mechanics* (January 23, 2017). https://www.popularmechanics.com/technology/infrastructure/a24692/fdr-new-deal-wpa-in- frastructure/

[32] Cory Booker, "Speech at the 2012 Democratic National Convention," *Huffington Post* (September 4, 2012). https://www.huffingtonpost.com/2012/09/04/cory-booker-speech-text-_n_1852212.html

[33] Blitz, "When America's Infrastructure Saved Democracy."

[34] Jim Powell, "How FDR's New Deal Harmed Millions of People," Cato Institute (December 29, 2003). https://www.cato.org/publications/commentary/how-fdrs-new-deal-harmed-millions-poor-people

[35] Tim Worstall, "The Case Against US Public Spending On Infrastructure," *Forbes* (February 29, 2016). https://www.forbes.com/sites/timworstall/2016/02/29/the-case-against-us-public-spending-on-infrastructure/#7f0526ba676c

[36] Amity Shlaes, "FDR Was a Great Leader, But His Economic Plan Isn't One to Follow," *Washington Post* (February 1, 2009). http://www.washingtonpost.com/wp-dyn/content/article/ 2009/01/30/AR2009013002760.html

[37] Ryan Bourne, "Five Bad Arguments for Public Infrastructure Spending," Foundation for Economic Education (April 13, 2017). https://fee.org/articles/5-bad-arguments-for-public-in- frastructure-spending/

[38] Ira Stoll, "Nine Reasons Government-Funded Infrastructure Is a Bad Idea," *Reason* (November 3, 2014). https://reason.com/archives/2014/11/03/why-government-funded-infrastructure-is

[39] William Press and Hunter Rawlings III, "Why Science? An Unemotional Argument for Federal Investment in Research," *Huffington Post* (June 20, 2014). https:// www.huffingtonpost.com/william-h-press/why-science-an-unemotiona_b_5515346.html

[40] Ibid.

CHAPTER NOTES

41. Michael White, "What Are the Benefits of Government-Funded Research?" *Pacific Standard* (July 18, 2014). https://psmag.com/news/benefits-government-funded-research-86168

42. Michael K. Evans, "The Economic Impact of NASA R&D Spending," Chase Econometrics (April 1976). https://ntrs.nasa.gov/archive/nasa/casi.ntrs.nasa.gov/19760017002.pdf

43. Phil Plait, "This is Why We Invest in Science. This." *Discover Magazine* (March 21, 2012). http://blogs.discovermagazine.com/badastronomy/2012/03/21/this-is-why-we-invest- in-science-this/#.XDzNEVVKiM8

44. Neil deGrasse Tyson, quoted in Chris Barth, "Invest In NASA, Invest In US Economy," *Forbes* (March 13, 20212). https://www.forbes.com/sites/chrisbarth/2012/03/13/neil-degrasse-tyson-invest-in-nasa-invest-in-u-s-economy/#64b962a515dc

45. Matt Ridley, "The Myth of Basic Science," Wall Street Journal (October 23, 2015). https://www.wsj.- com/articles/the-myth-of-basic-science-1445613954

46. Ibid.

47. Robert Lovell, "Darth Proxmire," *L-5 News* (November 1977). https://space.nss.org/media/L5- News-1977-11.pdf

48. Alexis Madrigal, "Moondoggle: The Forgotten Opposition to the Apollo Program," The Atlantic (September 12, 2012). https://www.theatlantic.com/technology/archive/2012/09/moondoggle- the-forgotten-opposition-to-the-apollo-program/262254/

49. "The History of Antitrust Regulations," Stanford University (accessed April 2019). https://cs.stanford.edu/people/er- oberts/cs181/projects/corporate-monopolies/government_history.html

50. Alex Samuels, "Uber, Lyft Return to Austin as Texas Gov. Abbott Signs Ride-Hailing Measure into Law," *Texas Tribune* (May 29, 2017). https://www.texastribune.org/2017/05/29/texas- gov-greg-abbott-signs-measure-creating-statewide-regulations-rid/

51. Tom Lehman, "Six Arguments Against Government Regulations," Capitalism (May 19, 2017). https://www.capitalism.com/six-arguments-government-regulations/

52. Ludwig Von Mises, *Socialism: An Economic and Sociological Analysis* (1922). Mises Institute (accessed April 2019). https://mises-medi-a.s3.amazonaws.com/Socialism percent20An percent20Economic percent20and percent20Socio-logical percent20Analysis_3.pdf?file=1&type=document

53. Lehman, "Six Arguments Against Government Regulations."

[54] Robert Crandall, "Extending Deregulation: Make the US Economy More Efficient," Brookings Institute (June 2016). https://www.brookings.edu/wp-content/uploads/2016/06/PB_Deregulation_Crandall.pdf

[55] "Trump's Deregulation Binge Is Lightening The Economy's Load," *Investor's Business Daily* (December 15, 2017). https://www.investors.com/politics/editorials/trumps-deregulation-binge/

[56] Michael Reagan, "Texas Economy Booms While California's Wheezes Along," Newsmax (July 29, 2017). https://www.newsmax.com/reagan/texas-california-gdp-job-creation/2017/07/29/id/ 804577/

[57] Victor Davis Hanson, "It's Still a Mad, Mad California," *National Review* (January 3, 2017). https://www.nationalreview.com/2017/01/california-madness-hypocritical-coastal-elites-soak- middle-class/

[58] Sidney Milkis, "Theodore Roosevelt: Impact and Legacy," UVA Miller Center (accessed April 2019). https://miller- center.org/president/roosevelt/impact-and-legacy

[59] "Government Regulation: Costs Lower, Benefits Greater Than Industry Estimates," Pew Trusts (May 26, 2015). https://www.pewtrusts.org/en/research-and-analysis/fact-sheets/2015/05/government-regulation-costs-lower-benefits-greater-than-industry-estimates

[60] Marc Davis, "Government Regulations: Do They Help Business?" Investopedia (October 5, 2018). https://www.investopedia.com/articles/economics/11/government-regulations.asp

[61] P.J. O'Rourke, "City Seminar: On the Wealth of Nations," Cato Institute (January 16, 2007). https://www.cato.org/publications/speeches/city-seminar-wealth-nations

[62] Jeff Foust, "New Policy Directive Implements Commercial Space Regulatory Reforms," *Space News* (May 24, 2018). https://spacenews.com/new-policy-directive-implements-commercial-space-regulatory-reforms/

INDEX

Addams, Jane, 12
Airline Deregulation Act (1978), 85
American Revolution, 7, 27, 47
American Taxpayer Relief Act (2012), 36
Appalachia, 14
ARPANET, 70
    See also Internet
atomic weapons, 66–67

B-29 bomber, 66–67
Bill and Melinda Gates Foundation, 78
Blue Origin, 97
Boaz, David, 30
Boeing, 68
Booker, Cory, 56
Brookings Institute, 38–40, 89–90
Buffet, Warren, 40
bull market, 41
Bush, George W., 19–20, 30–31
business tax, 26–27, 33

California, 29, 91–92
canals, 48, 50, 52–53
capitalism, 6–9, 11
Carson, Ben, 35
Carter, Jimmy, 86
Cato Institute, 20, 30, 33, 58
Center on Budget and Policy Priorities, 42
Centers for Disease Control and Prevention (CDC), 73
Chase Econometrics, 74
China, 16
Civil War, 47
Civilian Conservation Corps (CCC), 14
class warfare, 11–12
Clay, Henry, 47
Clayton Anti-Trust Act (1914), 84
Clinton, William, 20
Commercial Orbital Transportation Systems, 68
commercial space, 97–98
Commercial Spaceflight Federation, 98
communism, 8–9
competition, 7–8, 13, 21–22, 83–84, 88–89, 98
computers, 23
Conservative Party (UK), 10
conservatives, 42

Constitution, 62
Consumer Credit Protection Act (1969), 84
consumers, 7
corporate greed, 12, 84–85, 94, 96
corporate tax, 19, 21
CPA Journal, 20
Cruz, Ted, 35
Cumberland Road, 50–51

Defense Advance Research Projects Agency (DARPA), 69–70
Delaware, 29
democratic elections, 11
democratic socialism, 9–10, 38, 44
Denmark, 11
Department of Defense, 23, 69–70
Department of Energy, 23
deregulation, 21–24, 82, 85–93
discrimination, 83–84
Dodd-Frank Act, 23

Economic Opportunity Act (1964), 18
Economic Recovery Act (1981), 32–33
education, 11, 17–18, 38, 70, 80
efficiency, 88–90
Eisenhower, Dwight D., 51, 56
environment, 94–96
Environmental Protection Agency (EPA), 16, 85–86, 95–96
Erie Canal, 48, 50, 53
Executive Office of the President, 20

fairness, 94
Federal Aviation Administration (FAA), 85
Federal Communications Commission (FCC), 90
Federal Highway Act (1956), 56
Federal Reserve, 12, 39, 42
Federal Trade Commission, 84
Federal Writers' Project, 56
flat tax, 34–35
Forbes, Steve, 35
Ford, Gerald, 20
Foundation for Economic Education, 59–60
Franklin, Benjamin, 27
free market, 7–8, 17, 21–24, 88–90
French Revolution, 8
Friedman, Milton, 8, 32, 90

Furthering America's Research Enterprise, 72

Global Financial Crisis (2007-2011), 96
Golden Fleece Award, 79–80
government-funded projects
   arguments against, 58–62
   arguments for, 52–57
   examples of, 46–51
Great Britain, 9–10
Great Depression, 12–13, 55, 58–59, 66
Great Society, 15
greed, 11–12

Hamilton, Alexander, 52
Hanson, Victor Davis, 92
health care, 9–11, 94–96
Heritage Foundation, 16–17, 34–35
History Channel, 14–15
Hong Kong, 16–17, 33
Hoover Dam, 49, 56
Hoover Institute, 92
Howard Hughes Medical Institute, 78
Hudson River, 48

immigration, 80, 92, 96
income tax, 12, 19, 26–29, 33, 35, 37
Index of Economic Freedom, 16–17
inflation, 12, 32
infrastructure, 14–15, 46–58, 80
internal improvements, 52–54
   See also government-funded projects
Internal Revenue Service (IRS), 26, 28
   See also taxation; specific taxes
International Space Station, 68–69
Internet, 23, 70
Interstate Commerce Act (1887), 83
Interstate Commerce Commission, 83
inventions, 65–70, 74–75, 77–78

Jefferson, Thomas, 52
job training, 15, 18
John D. Rockefeller Foundation, 77
Johnson, Lyndon B., 15–16, 18–19

Kansas, 42–43
Kennedy, John F., 17, 19, 35, 37

Labour Party (UK), 9–10

libertarians, 62, 70
Lincoln, Abraham, 53–54
Löfven, Stefan, 10
Lyft, 86

Madison, James, 52
Manhattan Project, 66–67
Marx, Karl, 8–9
Meat Inspection Act (1906), 84
Medicaid, 38
Medicare, 38, 44
Michael J. Fox Foundation, 79
military, 64–66
Miller Center, 94
minorities, 80, 100
Mises, Ludwig von, 89
Mitchell, David, 33–34
mixed economy, 6, 11
monopolies, 82–83
Moon Express, 97
Musk, Elon, 50, 61

National Academy of Sciences, 72
National Advisory Committee on Aeronautics (NACA), 23, 66, 68
National Aeronautics and Space Administration (NASA), 23, 68–69, 72, 74–75, 79–80, 97
national debt, 38–40, 42
National Highway Administration, 56–57
National Institutes of Health, 24, 66
National Oceanic and Atmospheric Agency (NOAA), 69
National Science Foundation, 23, 67–68, 79
New Deal, 14–15, 51, 55, 58–59
New Jersey, 29
New York, 29, 48, 50
New York Stock Exchange, 41
Nixon, Richard, 16, 85
Norway, 11

Obama, Barack, 20, 35–36, 51
Ocasio-Cortez, Alexandria, 43–44
Occupational Safety and Health Administration (OSHA), 16, 86
Office of Naval Research, 80
Office of Science, 23
O'Rourke, P. J., 97

INDEX

Outer Space Treaty (1967), 98

Panama Canal, 51
Paul, Rand, 35
penicillin, 67, 78
Pew Research Center, 94–95
Pollock, Jackson, 56
poverty, 7, 9, 11–12, 15, 18–19, 80, 92–93
Press, William, 71–72
privately funded projects, 50–51, 61, 77–78
producers, 7
progressives, 11–14
property tax, 26–27
Proxmire, William, 79–80

QR Video
    consequences of not filing taxes, 28
    economic effects of deregulation, 84
    government and solar energy, 66
    New York's Erie Canal, 48
    origins of capitalism, 11

racism, 11–12, 100
Rawlings, Hunter, 71–72
Reagan, Ronald, 19, 21, 32–34, 39–40, 42
recession, 19, 21, 32–33
regulation, 12–17, 20–24, 82–85, 94–98
research and development, 23–24, 64–80
Revenue Act (1964), 37
Ridley, Matt, 77
Riss, Jacob, 12
robotics, 69
Rogers, Will, 27
Roosevelt, Franklin D., 13–15, 51, 55, 66
Roosevelt, Theodore, 12, 83, 94

safety, 12, 94–96
sales tax, 26–27
Sanders, Bernie, 9, 38, 44
Scandinavia, 11
science, 23, 64–80
Search for Extraterrestrial Intelligence (SETI), 80
Securities and Exchange Act (1934), 84
Securities and Exchange Commission (SEC), 14

Sherman Anti-Trust Act (1890), 83
Shlaes, Amity, 58–59
Smith, Adam, 7–8, 37, 88
Smithsonian Institution, 65
social democracy, 6, 9–15
Social Democratic Party (Sweden), 10
Social Security, 15, 38
social services, 9–11
socialism, 6, 8–11
Solow, Robert, 71
Soviet Union, 9
Space Policy Directive-2, 98
space program, 68–69, 72, 74, 79–80, 97–98
SpaceX, 50, 68, 97
states, 29, 42, 86–87, 91–92
Steinbeck, John, 56
STEM. *See* education
stimulus, 13–18
    and deregulation, 88–93
    and government research, 65–80
    and infrastructure, 52–62
    and regulation, 94–98
    and tax cuts, 30–40, 44
stock market, 12–13, 22–23, 96
subprime mortgage crisis, 22–23
subsidies, 15
Sweden, 10–11
Swenson, May, 56

Tarbell, Ida, 12
tax cuts, 17, 19–20
    arguments against, 38–43
    arguments for, 30–37
Tax Cuts and Jobs Act (2017), 39
Tax Reform Act (1986), 19, 40
taxation, 11–12, 16–21, 26–38
technology, 17, 23, 64–80
Tennessee Valley Authority (TVA), 14–15, 58
Tesla, 50
Texas, 86–87, 91–92
Thatcher, Margaret, 10
Transcontinental Railroad, 51, 54, 56
Trump, Donald, 20, 23, 38–39, 80, 90–91, 98
Truth in Packaging Act (1966), 84
Tyson, Neil deGrasse, 75

Uber, 50–51, 86
United States (US), 11

violence, 11–12

War on Poverty program, 15–19
Washington, George, 47
wasteful spending, 58–62, 77–80, 88–90
wealth, 7–9, 38–44
Wealth of Nations, The, 7–8, 88
welfare, 11, 38

West Virginia, 29
Wilson, Woodrow, 23, 84
Works Progress Administration (WPA), 14, 55–56, 59
World War I, 12, 56–57
World War II, 9, 16–17, 23, 56–57, 66–67
Worstall, Tim, 59

xenophobia, 12

AUTHOR'S BIOGRAPHY AND CREDITS

ABOUT THE AUTHOR

After working for twenty years as a computer analyst, Mark R. Whittington became a freelance writer. He has worked for Yahoo News and currently writes regularly for The Hill and the Daily Caller on public policy aspects of space exploration. He has been published in the *Wall Street Journal, Forbes, Business Insider, USA Today*, and the *Washington Post*, among other venues.

PICTURE CREDITS

Everett Historical: 13, 14, 53, 67; courtesy of the Friedman Foundation: 90; LBJ Library Photo: 18; National Aeronautics and Space Administration: 64; National Archives: 54; used under license from Shutterstock, Inc.: 1, 2, 22, 26, 49, 60, 70, 76, 85, 95; Rob Crandall / Shutterstock.com: 31; Sune Grabbe / Shutterstock.com: 10; Christopher Halloran / Shutterstock.com: 36; Jillian Cain Photography / Shutterstock.com: 93; photo.ua / Shutterstock.com: 41; Lev Radin / Shutterstock.com: 43; Mark Reinstein / Shutterstock.com: 21, 39; Bart Sadowski / Shutterstock.com: 6; Kenneth Sponsler / Shutterstock.com: 46; Mark Van Scyoc / Shutterstock.com: 82; Vince360 / Shutterstock.com: 61; Jonathan Weiss / Shutterstock.com: 78; Katherine Welles / Shutterstock.com: 73.

WITHDRAWN

$26.95

LONGWOOD PUBLIC LIBRARY
800 Middle Country Road
Middle Island, NY 11953
(631) 924-6400
longwoodlibrary.org

LIBRARY HOURS

Monday-Friday	9:30 a.m. - 9:00 p.m.
Saturday	9:30 a.m. - 5:00 p.m.
Sunday (Sept-June)	1:00 p.m. - 5:00 p.m.